THE FACTS ON
HALLOWEEN

JOHN ANKERBERG
JOHN WELDON &
DILLON BURROUGHS

HARVEST HOUSE PUBLISHERS
EUGENE, OREGON

Cover by Dugan Design Group, Bloomington, Minnesota

Cover photos © iStockphoto

Back cover author photo (Dillon) by Goldberg Photography

THE FACTS ON HALLOWEEN
Updated edition
Copyright © 1996/2008 by The John Ankerberg Theological Research Institute
Published by Harvest House Publishers
Eugene, Oregon 97408
www.harvesthousepublishers.com

Library of Congress Cataloging-in-Publication Data
    Ankerberg, John, 1945-
    The facts on Halloween / John Ankerberg, John Weldon ; updates by Dillon Burroughs.
        p. cm.—(The facts on)
    Includes bibliographical references.
    ISBN-13: 978-0-7369-2219-7 (pbk.)
    ISBN-10: 0-7369-2219-9 (pbk.)
    1. Halloween. 2. Amusements—Religious aspects—Christianity. 3. Christianity and culture. I. Weldon, John. II. Title.
    GT4965.A45 2006
    394.2646—dc22

                                                          2008001018

Printed in the United States of America

18 19 20 21 22 / BP-SK / 10 9 8 7 6 5

Contents

Trick or Treat?

Who doesn't remember the excitement and adventure of dressing up in their favorite costume to travel the neighborhood for as many pieces of candy as we could possibly scavenge? Adults and children alike enjoy joining in the festivities commonly known as Halloween.

In a marketing sense, Halloween has become big business today. The holiday is now the second most popular event for marketing activity, following Christmas. According to a National Retail Foundation survey, American consumers spent over $4.96 billion for Halloween in 2006, an average of $59.06 per person.[1] The National Confectioners Association reported in 2005 that 80 percent of adults planned to give out candy to trick-or-treaters, and that 93 percent of children planned to go trick-or-treating.[2] Even grown-ups are actively involved, as at least one in three adults will buy costumes for themselves. "Halloween has turned into the second- or third-biggest party night of the year, depending on who's counting, behind New Year's Eve and Super Bowl Sunday. Hallmark makes more than 300 Halloween cards."[3]

Who is driving the growth in Halloween? It's not older, affluent parents driving the surge in spending, but an increasing number of 18-to-24-year-olds. Among the 18-to-24-year-olds surveyed for the National Retail Federation by BIGresearch, responses were as follows:

85% said they planned to celebrate Halloween this year, up from 67% last year. Overall, 64% of adults surveyed said they would observe the holiday in some way, versus 53% last year. Nearly two-thirds of the 8,001 adults surveyed for the retailers group said they planned to pass out candy this year. About 30% said they would attend or throw a party, and 49% said they were planning to decorate their yard. Indeed, sales of decorations are expected to be the biggest mover, rising to $1.3 billion from $840 million last year.[4]

More than ever before, Halloween has become an enormously popular holiday. Interestingly, Halloween is also National Magic Day, observed worldwide by magicians, with even a National Magic Week observed the week of October 25 to 31.[5]

Halloween at work

Halloween is being embraced and observed in the workplace as never before. According to Human Resource Management's 2000 Benefits Study, more than one-third of U.S. companies offer some sort of workplace Halloween celebration.[6]

But many people have mixed feelings about the issue of Halloween. Do its pagan religious associations disqualify it spiritually or ethically as an activity that Christians can celebrate? In *The Facts on Halloween*, we'll investigate the origin of Halloween, its historic and contemporary relation to paganism and witchcraft, its symbols, and some of the mysteries commonly associated with Halloween, such as ghosts, haunted houses, and magic. We will also provide biblical and practical guidelines for evaluating Halloween from a Christian perspective.

Halloween—Ancient, Medieval, and Modern

1

What is the origin
of Halloween?

In AD 835, Pope Gregory IV designated November 1 as All Saints' Day, or All Hallows' Day (the term *hallow* refers to saints). The night before November 1, October 31, was known as All Hallows' Evening. How did we get the term *Halloween*? Look at the name "All Hallows' Evening." If we drop the word "all," the "s" on Hallows', and the "v" and "ing" on evening, the result spells *Halloween*.

Long before the church gave this name to the evening before All Saints' Day (a celebration in remembrance of saints and martyred saints), it had been celebrated in various ways in many places around the world. The book *Every Day's a Holiday* accurately observes that Halloween "probably combines more folk customs the world around than will ever be sorted out, catalogued and traced to their sources."[1]

The Druids

It is generally agreed by historians that Halloween came to take the place of a special day celebrated by the ancient Druids. The Druids were the educated or priestly class of the Celtic religion.[2] The Celts themselves were the first Aryan people who came from Asia to settle in Europe. In fact, we can see certain similarities between Druidism and the religion of India:

Celtic religion, presided over by the Druids (the priestly order) presents beliefs in various nature deities and certain ceremonies and practices that are similar to those in Indian religion. The insular Celts and the people of India also shared certain similarities of language and culture, thus indicating a common heritage.[3]

For example, the Indian pagan gods Siva Pasupati ("lord of the animals") and Savitr ("god of the sun") are similar to the Celtic gods Cernunnos, a horned god who appears in the yoga position, and the god Lug, or Lugus (perhaps originally a sun god). "As in Hinduism, the Druids also believed in reincarnation, specifically in the transmigration of the soul, which teaches that people may be reborn as animals."[4]

The Celtic peoples lived in northern France, throughout the United Kingdom, and in Ireland. They engaged in occult arts, worshiped nature, and gave nature supernatural, animistic qualities. Certain trees or plants, such as oak trees and mistletoe, were given great spiritual significance. (According to Celtic authority Lewis Spence, the original meaning of the term *Druid* implies a priest of the oak cult.) Interestingly, it has been claimed that 90 percent of the world's sometimes mysterious "crop circles" lie within the geographical proximity of the ancient and possibly Druidic ruins of Stonehenge. At least some of these phenomena may be considered supernatural.

What is the *occult*?

Religious writers often use the word *occult,* but what does it mean? According to the *Oxford American Dictionary, occult* can be defined as

1. secret, hidden except from those with more than

ordinary knowledge. 2. involving the supernatural,
occult powers. The occult [involves] the world of
the supernatural, mystical or magical.

In everyday usage, *occult* usually is used to refer to spiritual
practices that focus on secret knowledge gained through personal experience or attempts to communicate with spirits. The
term is used in reference to everything from ancient earth religions to modern conversations about ghosts and hauntings.[5]

The Celts worshiped the sun god Belenus, especially on *Beltane*, May 1, and they worshiped another
god, apparently the lord of death, or the lord of the
dead, on *Samhain* (pronounced "SOW-wen" by Wiccans), October 31. Beltane ("Fire of Bel") was the time
of the summer festival, while Samhain was the time of
the winter festival. Human sacrifice was offered during
both occasions. According to Julius Caesar in his *Commentaries* and other sources,[6] the Celts believed they
were descended from the god Dis, a tradition handed
down from the Druids. Dis was the Roman name for the
god of the dead.

Of the 400 names of Celtic gods known, Belenus is
mentioned most often. *Samhain* as the specific name
of the lord of death is uncertain, but it is possible that
the lord of death was the chief Druid deity. We'll follow
the common practice of other authors on this issue and
refer to this deity by the name Samhain.

Druidic festivals

The Celts and their Druid priests began their New
Year on November 1, which marked the beginning of
winter. They apparently believed that on October 31,
the night before their New Year and the last day of the
old year, Samhain gathered the souls of the evil dead

who had been condemned to enter the bodies of animals. He then decided what animal form they would take for the next year. (The souls of the good dead were reincarnated as humans.) The Druids also believed that the punishment of the evil dead could be lightened by sacrifices, prayers, and gifts to Samhain.

Druid worshipers attempted to satisfy and please this deity because of his power over the souls of the dead, whether these souls were good or evil. For those who had died during the preceding 12 months, Samhain allowed their spirits to return to earth to their former places of habitation for a few hours to associate once again with their families.[7]

As a result of this belief, the Celts taught that on their New Year's Eve (our Halloween) ghosts, evil spirits, and witches roamed the earth. In order to honor the sun god (Belenus) and to frighten away evil spirits who allegedly feared fire, large bonfires were lit on hilltops. In Lewis Spence's *The History and Origins of Druidism* we read,

> The outstanding feature of *Samhain* was the burning of a great fire....*Samhain* was also a festival of the dead, whose spirits at this season were thought of as scouring the countryside, causing dread to the folk at large. To expel them from the fields and the precincts of villages, lighted brands from the bonfire were carried around the district...Divinations for the fate of the individual throughout the new year were engaged in.[8]

For several days before New Year's Eve (October 31), young boys would travel the neighborhood begging for material to build these massive bonfires. The fires were believed to not only banish evil spirits but rejuvenate the sun. Until fairly recent times, the hilltop Halloween fires of the Scots were called *Samhnagan*, indicating the lingering influence of the ancient Celtic festival.[9]

On this night, evil or frustrated ghosts were also believed to play tricks on humans and cause supernatural manifestations, just like poltergeists today. As part of the celebration, people dressed in grotesque masks and danced around the great bonfires, often pretending they were being pursued by evil spirits. In addition, food was put out to make the ghosts or souls of the good dead Samhain had released feel welcomed and at home. Because Samhain marked the beginning of a new year, an interest in divination (the magic art of interpreting the unknown by interpreting random patterns or symbols) and fortune-telling became an important part of this holiday.

For example, the Druids believed that the particular shape of various fruits and vegetables could help predict, or divine, the future. Victims of human sacrifice were used for the same purpose. When the Romans conquered Britain, some of their customs were added to the traditions of the Druids, while others, such as human sacrifice, were banned.

The Samhain celebration was not unique to the Druids. Many festivals worldwide celebrate a time when the dead return to mingle with the living. The Hindus call it a night of Holi. The Iroquois Native Americans celebrate a feast of the dead every 12 years, when all those who have died during the preceding 12 years are honored with prayers. A national holiday in Mexico, the Day of the Dead, begins on November 2 and lasts several days. In this gruesome festival, death becomes a kind of neighborly figure, appearing on candy, jewelry, toys, bread, cakes, and so on. This is the time when the souls of the dead return and when the living are to honor them. For example, doors are decorated with flowers to welcome the *angelitos*, the souls of dead children.

For the most part, then, our modern Halloween appears to trace its initial origin to the practices of the ancient Druids at their winter festival on October 31.

2

Are the specific customs of Halloween related to pagan beliefs?

Since Halloween itself originated in paganism, it is not surprising that its customs are related to pagan belief. According to the *Encyclopaedia Britannica*,

> In ancient Britain and Ireland, the Celtic Festival of Samhain was observed on October 31, at the end of summer.... The souls of the dead were supposed to revisit their homes on this day and the autumnal festival acquired sinister significance, with ghosts, witches, goblins, black cats, fairies and demons of all kinds said to be roaming about. It was the time to placate the supernatural powers controlling the processes of nature. In addition, Halloween was thought to be the most favorable time for divinations concerning marriage, luck, health, and death. It was the only day on which the help of the devil was invoked for such purposes.[10]

Halloween symbols, customs, and practices undoubtedly have had a variety of influences upon Western culture throughout history. However, in early American history, Halloween was not celebrated due to America's strong Christian heritage. It was not widely observed until the twentieth century. Initially, it was practiced only in small Irish Catholic settlements, until thousands of Irish migrated to America during the great potato famine and brought their customs with them. To some degree, our modern Halloween is an Irish holiday with early origins in the Celtic winter festival. Interestingly, in American culture, the rise in popularity of Halloween also coincides roughly with the national rise in spiritism that began in 1848.[11]

Irish holiday

Ireland is the only place in the world where Halloween is actually a national holiday (celebrated with fireworks); children are even released from school for the week.

Among the modern customs and practices of Halloween, we can note numerous probable or possible influences, some of which follow.

Where did the jack-o'-lantern originate?

The carved pumpkin may have originated with the witches' use of a collection of skulls with a candle in each to light the way to coven meetings. But among the Irish, who, as noted, prompted the popularization of Halloween in America, the legend of "Irish Jack" explains the jack-o'-lantern. According to the legend, a stingy drunk named Jack tricked the devil into climbing an apple tree for an apple, but then cut the sign of a cross into the trunk of the tree to prevent the devil from coming down. Jack then forced the devil to swear he would never come after Jack's soul. The devil reluctantly agreed.

Jack eventually died, but he was turned away at the gates of heaven because of his drunkenness and life of selfishness. He was sent to the devil, who also rejected him, keeping his promise. Since Jack had no place to go, he was condemned to wander the earth. As he was leaving hell (he happened to be eating a turnip), the devil threw a live coal at him. He put the coal inside the turnip and has since forever been roaming the earth with his "jack-o'-lantern" in search of a place to rest. Eventually, pumpkins replaced turnips since it was much easier to symbolize the devil's coal inside a pumpkin.

How did the tradition of trick-or-treating begin?

There are several ancient practices that point to this tradition. One possibility is from the notion that ancient witches had to steal the materials needed for their festivals. The Druids may have believed that witches held this day to be special, something clearly true for modern witches.

The idea of trick-or-treating is further related to the ghosts of the dead in pagan, and even Catholic, history. For example, among the ancient Druids, "The ghosts that were thought to throng about the houses of the living were greeted with a banquet-laden table. At the end of the feast, masked and costumed villagers representing the souls of the dead paraded to the outskirts of town leading the ghosts away."[12]

As already noted, Halloween was thought to be a night when mischievous and evil spirits roamed freely. As in modern poltergeist lore, mischievous spirits could play tricks on the living—so it was advantageous to "hide" from them by wearing costumes. Masks and costumes were worn to either scare away the ghosts or to keep from being recognized by them:

In Ireland especially, people thought that ghosts and spirits roamed after dark on Halloween. They lit candles or lanterns to keep the spirits away, and if they had to go outside, they wore costumes and masks to frighten the spirits or to keep from being recognized by these unearthly beings.[13]

Where did Halloween costumes originate?

Besides the reasons given above, Halloween masks and costumes were used to hide one's attendance at pagan festivals or—as in traditional shamanism (mediated by a witch doctor or pagan priest) and other forms of animism—to change the personality of the wearer to allow for communication with the spirit world. Here, costumes could be worn to ward off evil spirits. On the other hand, the costume wearer might use a mask to try to attract and absorb the power of the animal represented by the mask and costume worn. According to this scenario, Halloween costumes may have originated with the Celtic Druid ceremonial participants, who wore animal heads and skins to acquire the strength of a particular animal.

An additional layer of tradition explaining the origin of Halloween costumes comes from the medieval Catholic practice of displaying the relics of saints on All Saints' Day: "The poorer churches could not afford relics and so instituted a procession with parishioners dressed as the patron saints; the extras dressed as angels or devils and everyone paraded around the churchyard."[14]

Going from door to door seeking treats may result from the Druidic practice of begging material for the great bonfires. As we will see later, it is also related to the Catholic concept of purgatory and the custom of begging for a "soul cake."

As for the "trick" custom of Halloween, this is related to the idea that ghosts and witches created mischief on this particular night. For example, if the living did not provide food, or "treats," for the spirits, then the spirits would "trick" the living. People feared terrible things might happen to them if they did not honor the spirits. The Druids also believed that failure to worship their gods would bring dire consequences. If the gods were not treated properly in ritual, they would seek vengeance. This was therefore a day of fear. Further, some people soon realized that a mischievous sense of humor, or even malevolence, could be camouflaged—that they could perform practical jokes on or do harm to others and blame it on the ghosts or witches roaming about.

What's the significance of fruits and nuts at Halloween?

Halloween traditions often involve fruit centerpieces, apples, and nuts. Three of the sacred fruits of the Celts were acorns, apples, and nuts, especially the hazelnut, considered a god, and the acorn, sacred from its association to the oak. Fruits and nuts also seem to be related to the Roman harvest feast of Pomona, apparently the goddess of fruit. For example, in ancient Rome, cider was drawn and the Romans bobbed for apples, which was part of a divination that supposedly helped a person discover their future marriage partner.

How did we get the tradition of telling ghost stories?

It became a natural expression of Halloween to tell ghost stories when dead souls were believed to be everywhere, and good, mischievous, and evil spirits roamed freely. These stories further originated as a personal expression of these beliefs.

3

How does Halloween relate historically to the Roman Catholic Church, the dead, and purgatory?

In the Dark Ages and Early Middle Ages, the Catholic Church attempted to oppose the paganism involved in the Samhain festival by making November 1 All Saints' Day and November 2 All Souls' Day. As noted, All Saints' Day was a remembrance and celebration of the saints, especially the ones who were heroic martyrs (people who died for their faith). All Souls' Day became a day on which Roman Catholics prayed for the dead in order to help them escape the torments of purgatory.

In the year AD 609 or 610, Pope Boniface IV grievously strayed from biblical teaching by dedicating the Roman Pantheon, formerly a pagan temple to every known god, to the Virgin Mary and all Christian martyrs. This was done on May 13, a day that became a feast day. In 835 Pope Gregory IV transferred this feast to November 1 and extended it to include all of the saints.[15] As a result, November 1, All Saints' Day, the day after Halloween (Hallows' Eve or All Saints' Eve), became a day dedicated by the Catholic Church to the Virgin Mary and the saints.* Eventually, November 2 evolved into All Souls' Day, a special day to pray for the dead. As we will see, this custom supposedly originated

---

* The 1987 edition of *The Catholic Encyclopedia* gives an alternate history. It states that Pope Boniface IV (died 615) instituted the All Saints' Feast in the West, and Gregory III consecrated a chapel in St. Peter's Basilica in honor of all the saints and set the date of the feast.

with a mystical vision of the Catholic Saint Odilo, who died in 1048.

Helping the dead

Unfortunately, reminiscent of the ancient Druids, the Roman Catholic Church still teaches that the living can help relieve the sufferings of the dead through various acts. For example, a person can supposedly pray for souls being tormented in purgatory and ease their pains through specific or sacrificial acts such as penance, partaking of the sacraments, mortification, using the rosary, good deeds, and almsgiving. Special attention is given to prayers toward the Virgin Mary, who is believed to have the power to release the suffering from purgatory. The Catholic concept of purgatory has many parallels in other religions, but we must strongly emphasize that the idea of purgatory is not mentioned at all in the Bible.[16] The idea of praying to the Virgin Mary or praying for the dead is neither biblical nor Christian.[*]

Masses for the dead

The Catholic saint Odilo was Abbot of Cluny. He had a vision, similar to other Catholic saints or mystics, of souls suffering terribly in purgatory. This vision led him to the unbiblical practice of having special masses said on the behalf of these souls in all the churches affiliated with Cluny. This new practice soon spread.[18]

An article in *U.S. Catholic* observes, "By the end of the thirteenth century, All Souls' Day on November 2nd had become a set feast day to pray for our dead throughout the Latin church." The article points out that Halloween, All Saints' Day, and All Souls' Day are

---

[*] The distressing consequences of these unbiblical beliefs are clearly illustrated in books such as *The Facts on Roman Catholicism*.[17]

days to concentrate on, in this order: sin, sanctification, and the dead:

> And on November 2, All Souls' Day, let's hope some people will go to the cemetery or to a church and pray for us, their dead. Halloween, All Saints' Day, All Souls' Day—October 31st, November 1st, November 2nd—all are feast days and All Saints' Day is a holy day of obligation. We must admit that we are sinners, that we are obliged to honor the saints and are called to be saints ourselves, and that it is our duty to remember our dead, the faithful departed.[19]

Similar beliefs among Druids and Roman Catholics

As noted, it was the ancient pagan Druids who believed in a purgatory-like concept:

> The Celts believed that the sinful souls of those who had died during the year had been relegated to the bodies of animals. Through gifts and sacrifices their sins could be expiated and the souls freed to claim a heavenly reward. Samhain judged the souls and decreed in what form their existence was to continue, whether in the body of a human being or in an animal.[20]

Yet there are additional historic and contemporary examples of how Halloween and purgatory evolved from pagan practices and are related:

- In the late 1800s, it was customary for English Catholics to assemble at midnight on Halloween and pray for the souls of their departed friends. "The custom was observed in every Catholic farm in the district, but was gradually given up."[21] One individual reported in November 1909 that his grandfather would light a bundle of straw and throw it into the air with his pitchfork; short prayers were said while the straw was lit and thrown. When asked about it, "my grandfather replied that it was to represent the holy souls escaping from Purgatory to Heaven."[22] A probing response could be to ask, "Is there a place in the Bible that promotes this view?"

- On November 2 in Belgium, people eat special "All Souls' cakes" because, supposedly, "the more cakes you eat on this night, the more souls you can save from Purgatory."[23] Where does the Bible suggest this?

- "In Sicily, on All Souls' Day, cakes with images of skulls and skeletons are eaten."[24]

- A popular Halloween song in the Philippines goes, "…ordinary souls we are, from Purgatory we have come. And there we are duty-bound to pray by night and day. If alms you are to give, be in a hurry please for the door of heaven may close on us forever."[25] Jesus is the only one who holds the keys to the door of heaven. He promises to open it to anyone who puts their trust in him to be their only Savior from sin.

- In France, All Souls' Day (*Le Jour des Morts*) "is dedicated to prayers for the dead who are not yet glorified."[26]

- Ruth Hutchison and Ruth Adams report that in earlier times people took special loaves of bread called "souls" to the cemeteries, placing them on the graves. The people ate these "soul cakes" because they were thought to serve as a powerful antidote against any flames of purgatory "that might be invoked by returning ghosts. At dusk the festival changed from All Saints' Day to All Souls' Eve. Lighted candles were placed on graves and in windows, to guide the dead back home."[27]

- In the Middle Ages on All Souls' Day, the poor would go begging for soul cakes, which could be given as payment for prayers they had promised to say for the dead.[28]

These examples illustrate how Halloween is related both to ancient Celtic practice and the Catholic concept of purgatory. Significantly, the Lutheran Church dedicated October 31, or the Sunday nearest it, to be the date commemorating the beginning of the Protestant Reformation. In Martin Luther's time, the corrupt practice of buying indulgences for the dead "suffering in purgatory" was common. Appropriately, in 1517, on Halloween day itself, Luther took his 95 Theses, which attacked the concept of selling indulgences to free those in purgatory, and nailed them to the castle church door in Wittenberg, Germany.[29]

4

Is Halloween related to modern pagan practices?

In spite of the historical evidence for the origin of Halloween practices, Halloween today is assumed to be an innocent time for most children. However, it is a very serious observance for many witches, neopagans, and other similar religious groups. Before we proceed, it should be noted that the historic and contemporary spiritual associations to Halloween have produced something of a crossover effect to the larger society so that in some instances even the observance of Halloween is not a seemingly innocent practice. In reading through various histories of Halloween, it is surprising to notice the large number of superstitions and divination practices involved. There can be no doubt that many of these practices and beliefs can be directly related to the practices of pagan religions.

Divination

Of special concern is how pagan beliefs and superstitions may regulate or control a person's life in unhealthy ways. True divination almost always brings harmful consequences.* Since the last quarter of the nineteenth century, Halloween has been regarded as a time "for working charms, spells, and divinations."[30]

Christians should not indulge in such practices, as God says in the Bible:

> Let no one be found among you…who practices divination or sorcery, interprets omens, engages in witchcraft, or casts spells, or who is a medium or spiritist or who consults the dead. Anyone who does these things is detestable to the LORD (Deuteronomy 18:10-12).

As we noted earlier, this may be related to the ancient Druids since Samhain marked the beginning of the new year, which resulted in an interest in divination and fortune-telling to discover what the coming year would bring.

On Halloween, it was believed (and still is in some places) that following a particular ritual may allow an

---

* This topic is discussed in our *Encyclopedia of New Age Beliefs* (Harvest House Publishers, 1996).

apparition of a person's future mate to appear behind you:

> Many beliefs arose about how to conjure up the image of one's future wife or husband. Girls believed that if one sat at midnight before a mirror eating an apple, the image of her future husband would suddenly appear before her. If no image appeared it was taken to mean that the girl would remain a spinster.[31]

In Ireland, it was believed that "on Hallow Eve Night the spirits of the dead rise and go on the earth, girls at the hearth play at divining the identities of future mates, and in the past boys dressed in suits of white straw and caroused over the hills in the company of the dead, attacking the homes of men who kept their daughters from the cohort of bachelors."[32] Other divination beliefs that were practiced included, "an apple peeling thrown over the left shoulder will curve into the initial of the one you will marry."[33]

In the New World

"The use of nuts for divination was so common that even in America Halloween was once known as 'Nutcrack Night.'"[34]

In Scotland, "If a girl went into her room at midnight on the fatal eve [Halloween] and sat down before her mirror and cut an apple into nine slices and held each slice on the point of her knife before eating it she might see in the mirror looking over her shoulder the face of her future lover and he would ask for the last slice."[35] As we've noted, the pagan use of fruits and nuts for divination on Halloween was borrowed from the Celts and Romans.

Further, Halloween has also become a common day for children to use a Ouija board or another device for divining in an attempt to contact the ghosts and spirits that are believed to be roaming the earth. Yet Ouija boards are biblically forbidden and anything but an innocent pastime. They can lead to serious psychological and spiritual consequences, including spirit-possession.*

Divination, in the sense of obtaining secret knowledge about a person's future death, has historically been practiced on Halloween and continues to be today. On Halloween in North Wales, for instance, each family built a large bonfire near their house. The fire, called *Coel Coeth*, became a means of divination. Each member of the house would throw a white stone into the fire that was marked for later identification. In the morning they returned to the ashes in search of their stones. "If any stone was missing, the Welshman believed that its owner would not live to see another Halloween." Others believed that if a person ate a crust of dry bread before going to bed on Halloween, his wish would be fulfilled.[36]

In the southern United States, there is a custom based on the terrible Druidic belief that the struggles of victims of human sacrifice revealed omens of the future:

> Alcohol was put in a bowl and lighted and "fortunes" in the shape of figs, orange peel, raisins, almonds and dates, wrapped in tin foil, were thrown into the flame. The girl who snatched out of the burning the best thing would meet her future husband within a year.[37]

Under the subheading of "Halloween Charms," one popular book for children even gives a description of

---

* Documented in our *Encyclopedia of New Age Beliefs*.

British customs involving rituals for divining different aspects of one's future.[38]

The concern over such activities can be seen in the following statement from the *American Book of Days:* "Various methods of divining the future were used on Halloween and the results were accepted in all seriousness."[39] In other words, when we are dealing with a sober approach to divining the future—with subjects such as overall fortune, marriage partners, or life and death—it can open the world to spirit contact, or lead to spiritual consequences in our lives that may be much more serious than mere games.

Today, similar practices are observed on Halloween. In New Orleans, "the Voodoo Museum usually offers a special Halloween ritual in which people may see true voodoo rites." In Salem, Massachusetts, a Halloween festival occurs from October 13 to 31 and includes a psychic fair.[40] The explosive growth of the Harry Potter children's book series and the related popularity of similar books and films has also increased cultural acceptance of such pagan beliefs.

A night special in witchcraft and Satanism

In contemporary witchcraft, Halloween is considered a very special night. A standard book on neopaganism singles out three dates as the key celebration days for witchcraft:

> The greater sabbats are: *Samhain* (Halloween or November Eve), the Celtic New Year; the days when the walls between the worlds were said to be thinnest and when contact with one's ancestors took place; *Oimelc* (February 1), the winter purification festival… *Beltane* (May 1), the great fertility festival…. Different Craft traditions…treat the festivals in diverse ways.

But almost all traditions at least celebrate Samhain and Beltane.[41]

Some witches request a day off from work for their special day, while others have actually sought to have schools closed to commemorate their great sabbat. In 2004, the Puyallup, Washington, school district even banned Halloween from schools out of fear of offending local Wiccans.[42]

Many satanic groups also consider Halloween a special night in part because Halloween "became the only day of the year in which it was believed that the devil could be invoked for help in finding out about future marriages, health, deaths, crops, and what was to happen in the new year."[43] Though they are two different religious movements, contemporary witchcraft and Satanism share certain characteristics. While they are distinct entities and modern witchcraft and Wicca deny the existence of Satan, there remains clear biblical precedent that the devil is the spiritual source of power behind the beliefs and practices of witchcraft, Satanism, and other similar movements.[44] Former witch Doreen Irvine observes, "Witchcraft of the black kind is not far removed from Satanism…Black witches have great power and are not to be taken lightly…They [may] exhume fresh graves and offer the bodies in sacrifice to Satan."[45]

In addition, claims have been made that human sacrifices have taken place among certain Satanist groups.[46] Similar human sacrifice also occurred regularly among the Druids. According to Roman historian Tacitus, the Druids "covered their altars with the blood" of victims, mostly criminals. According to Caesar, human sacrifice was a common and frequent element in Druidism. In large cages, scores of people were burned alive at once; the larger the number of victims, the greater the yield of crops. But if the gods were not appeased by the sacrifice of criminals, innocent victims were also offered. According to Lucan, a first-century Latin poet, three Celt gods in particular were hungry for human souls— Teutates, Esus, and Taranis.[47]

We noted earlier that the struggles of the dying victims were held to contain knowledge of the future. The Druids had full confidence in human sacrifice as a method of divination. According to Spence,

> Horrible indeed was the method by which the Druids divined future events after a human sacrifice. "The Druids," says Tacitus, "consult the gods in the palpitating entrails of men," while Strabo informs us that they stabbed a human victim in the back with a sword and then drew omens from the convulsive movements made by him in his death-struggles. Diodorus says that they augured from the posture in which the victim fell, from his contortions, and the direction in which the blood flowed from the body. From these, "they formed their predictions according to certain rules left them by their ancestors."[48]

We will discuss the relationship between witchcraft and Halloween later. However, it is clear from these historical facts that the Halloween of past and present is based in pagan occult practices that are condemned in the Bible, and should be viewed as something much more serious than merely a day for children's trick or treating.

A Christian and Biblical Analysis of Halloween

5

Can Halloween be an
entirely innocent practice?

To ask the question another way, is it all right for Christians to participate in Halloween? We are not suggesting that Christians who choose to participate in Halloween are necessarily sinning, but it is important to investigate whether involvement in Halloween's practices is honoring to God. Our hope is that you will take a closer look at your personal involvement, based on the following discussion.

Not everything in life is clear-cut or has an easy answer. However, when it comes to making a choice on whether to participate in Halloween, our advice, based on biblical teaching, is to urge you to abstain from Halloween traditions. Why? Based on our research, we have discovered that Halloween symbolism and activities today, though technically removed from their ancient practices, continue to *retain the underlying associations* for which they were intended.

Just costumes?

What is the reason children dress up as witches, ghosts, or demons on Halloween? What does God think about dressing up our children to represent these entities?

Five issues to think over

As you evaluate this issue, here are some questions and comments to consider.

1. Who might be influenced? If we innocently align ourselves with something that has been and continues to be connected with spiritual evil, can we be certain we will never be affected? In merely participating in Halloween, are we ignorantly involving ourselves in practices that dishonor God and associating ourselves with all he hates? Historically, how can we ignore the facts that indicate Halloween is the very day that the dark powers have chosen for themselves as special above all others—from the ancient Druids to modern Druids, witches, and Satanists?

Unfortunately, isn't it also true that most Christians don't even know these facts? But if the purpose of following Christ is to glorify God, is it really possible to glorify him by imitating, however innocently, what non-Christian religions do on their special day? Should Christians set out to imitate the things that historically *and* today are traced to something evil or dark, including dressing in costumes, trick-or-treating, displaying decorations, and setting out displays of fruit? As we have already shared, setting out fruit and other food had a special purpose:

> Appeasement of the spirits was celebrated in various ways according to locale and custom, with minor differences. One way to appease the dead was to set out bowls of fruit and other treats so they could partake of them and, once satisfied, they would leave in peace. Your child, when he goes door to door in the ritual of "trick or treat," is reenacting the ancient superstition.[1]

Dressing in costumes or collecting candy are certainly neutral practices on any other day, such as at costume parties. So it is not *the practices, but rather their association* to this particular day and their original purpose that raises the issue of involvement. Does this mean it is wrong for a parent to take their child out dressed as Spider-Man or a princess to a few friends' houses in the neighborhood for some candy? We are not suggesting this is a sinful act, only that it is probably not the best choice.

Even many Christian scholars who oppose Halloween altogether aren't sure whether something like this falls under the individual conscience prescriptions in 1 Corinthians 10:23-29 and Romans 14. Views have ranged from little concern regarding Halloween involvement to complete abstinence from the holiday. Many churches have sought to offer healthier alternatives through church-sponsored harvest parties or similar events on Halloween night. Others have chosen the night to host a churchwide prayer meeting.

However, even with partial involvement, are we still celebrating or honoring Halloween in a sense? Based on everything we know of Halloween, 1 Corinthians 10:23-24 seems to suggest that abstinence is the best option:

> "Everything is permissible"—but not everything is beneficial. "Everything is permissible"—but not everything is constructive. Nobody should seek his own good, but the good of others.

2. *Mimicking evil practices?* Most people think that imitating these things on Halloween is innocent since we do not believe in the original practices or intent. However, the Bible repeatedly shares with us not to *imitate* the evil practices of the surrounding sinful culture. For example, when 3 John 11 says, "Do not *imitate* what is evil," it means to not copy it or act it out. A.T. Robertson's *Word Pictures of the Greek New Testament*

points out that the Greek word for "do not imitate" (*mé mimou*) is the present middle imperative of prohibition, meaning, "do not have the habit of imitating." It comes from *mimeomai*, which means a mimic or an actor. This Scripture seems to teach that we are not even to *mimic*, act out, or copy the ancient practices of Halloween. Wouldn't this also apply to the current activities of the holiday? Isn't participation a form of imitation? And doesn't our participation say something to others?

3. *Giving credence?* In partaking of Halloween, do we help, even indirectly, publicize what may be the single most important day in the world of the dark and evil spirits? By our participation, do we give at least some credence to the celebration of evil simply because we participate in a day that originates in the world of evil spiritual practices?

4. *Exposing our children?* Can we, even indirectly, be setting up our children to become familiar with the practices of spiritual darkness? Isn't it true that even if our own children are dressed in positive and innocent costumes, they are in the midst of other people (children and adults) who are dressed up as witches, sorcerers, the devil, demons, ghosts, and other dark themes? It is impossible for our children to avoid this. Could this exposure cause some of our children to feel comfortable exploring occult areas in the future? When our children ask us *why* kids dress up in costumes and why they trick or treat, wondering where such practices came from, can we give them any other answer that is not tied back to non-Christian, occult, evil practices?

5. *So how about the dark side?* Isn't it also true that, besides getting lots of candy, many children enjoy Halloween

for the "trick" aspect of it, fascinated with scaring other people? In extreme cases, young people even use the excuse of Halloween to participate in vandalism and arson. In this sense, aren't they imitating the ancient evil spirits that Samhain released on Halloween Eve? Do we want our children involved on this particular night when others are out to cause fear or destruction?

And aren't many other children secretly fascinated by the scary and evil side of Halloween—witches, ghosts, demons, goblins, graves, dead bodies, and other forbidden things? Is this in harmony with what we read in Philippians 4:8—"Finally, brothers, whatever is true, whatever is noble, whatever is right, whatever is pure, whatever is lovely, whatever is admirable—if anything is excellent or praiseworthy—think about such things"? When the apostle Paul tells us we are to be imitators of God, and of him as he is the imitator of Jesus, can we be imitators of God and godliness when we imitate the practices of spiritual darkness on Halloween night? If the apostle Paul lived today, what do you think he would say about Halloween?

To put it another way, can we pretend we are not part of something when we cannot totally avoid it? If it is impossible to participate in Halloween innocently *because* of the very nature of Halloween day and its implications, how can we logically think we aren't, at least in some sense, part of what it represents when we participate in any part of it?

What the Bible has to say

Now, let's look at some Scriptures, some of which we've already referred to, to see what bearing they may have upon Halloween:

Follow my example, as I follow the example of Christ (1 Corinthians 11:1).

Be imitators of God, therefore, as dearly loved children and live a life of love, just as Christ loved us and gave himself up for us as a fragrant offering and sacrifice to God. But among you *there must not be even a hint* of sexual immorality, or of any kind of impurity, or of greed, because *these are improper for God's holy people* (Ephesians 5:1-3).

When you enter the land the LORD your God is giving you, *do not learn to imitate* the detestable ways of the nations there (Deuteronomy 18:9).

Hear what the LORD says to you...*do not learn the ways* of the nations...For the customs of the peoples are worthless (Jeremiah 10:1-3).

Do not be yoked together with unbelievers. For what do righteousness and wickedness have in common? Or what fellowship can light have with darkness? What harmony is there between Christ and Belial [the devil]? *What does a believer have in common with an unbeliever?* What agreement is there between the temple of God and idols? For we are the temple of the living God. As God has said: "I will live with them and walk among them, and I will be their God, and they will be my people. Therefore *come out from them and be separate,*" says the Lord. "*Touch no unclean thing,* and I will receive you. I will be a Father to you, and you will be my sons and daughters," says the Lord Almighty (2 Corinthians 6:14-18).

Hate what is evil; cling to what is good (Romans 12:9).

Avoid every kind of evil (1 Thessalonians 5:22).

Do not imitate what is evil (3 John 11).

Live as children of light (for the fruit of the light consists in all goodness, righteousness and truth) and *find out*

> *what pleases the Lord.* Have *nothing to do* with the fruitless
> deeds of darkness, but rather expose them (Ephesians
> 5:8-11).

Do you think these Scriptures relate to the issue of
Christian participation in Halloween? Is it possible
to avoid every kind of evil (or "appearance of evil" in
the King James version) and also send our children out
dressed as devils, demons, or ghosts? Is it possible to not
imitate or learn evil while wearing and learning modern
symbols of ancient evil practices—especially for our
children? Is it possible to have nothing to do with the
fruitless deeds of darkness and still participate in Halloween? The apostle John wrote, "This is the message we
have heard from him and declare to you: God is light;
in him *there is no darkness at all.* If we claim to have
fellowship with him yet walk in darkness, we lie and
do not live by the truth" (1 John 1:5-6). Cannot Halloween be considered, at least in some sense, "walking
in the darkness"?

Learning the good. When the Bible tells us we are not
to learn the ways of the pagan nations, but are to learn
that which is good (Deuteronomy 18:9; Hebrews 13:7;
3 John 11), we must think of the word "learn" according
to the definition given by A.T. Robertson in his *Word
Pictures of the New Testament:*

> The directing of one's mind to something and producing
> an external effect, learn; 1) as learning through instruc-
> tion, be taught, learn from someone (John 7:15); 2) as
> learning through inquiry, ascertain, discover, find out
> (Acts 23:27); 3) as learning through practice or experi-
> ence, come to know, come to realize (Philippians 4:11;
> Hebrews 5:8); 4) as achieving comprehension, under-
> stand, learn (Revelation 14:3).

This is the sense in which we should understand Deuteronomy 5:1: "Moses summoned all Israel, and said: 'Hear, O Israel, the decrees and laws I declare in your hearing today. Learn them and be sure to follow them.'" The issue then, is whether our children are imitating and learning something they shouldn't on Halloween. If we are instructed to learn about what is good and not to teach our children to follow pagan practices, then we can't use ignorance of such practices and beliefs as an excuse for our participation.

How does God, as he looks down on Halloween night in full awareness of the events that have happened throughout history, view little children, especially Christian children, dressed up as ghosts, devils, witches, and goblins? Even if they are dressed as innocent characters, how does God view Christian parents, his own spiritual children, participating in an event that on that very day is so honored by Satan—the day on which so much evil has been committed historically, and still is being committed on that very night?

Keeping the wrong company

If the Ku Klux Klan had a special day, would Christian parents dress up their kids as klansmen and send them out at night to commemorate it, even in fun and jest? Of course not! Why? Because parents would not want their children associated with the negative acts this organization characterizes.

Honoring God

All of this raises an even larger question. Does the fact that Christians participate in Halloween dishonor God and honor the work of Satan? Again, what does God think of his little children walking around involved in the very symbolism of the day that Satanists, ancient pagan religions, and those practicing witchcraft have claimed as their most sacred day of the year? Or the night that human sacrifices of children have occurred on? Is it possible we can see Satan deliberately mocking God by having children actively participate in the symbolic activities on the very day which he, Satan, is most honored?

Satan, of course, knows the meanings of these symbols—and so does God. If we think of who Satan is, what he does, and how *he* views Halloween, then how must God view little children being out on Halloween, Satan's special day—even being sent out by Christian parents? Perhaps then it doesn't seem so innocent anymore.

Satan is very real and is out to cause trouble among children. In contrast, Jesus loved children and said of them that "the kingdom of heaven belongs to such as these" (Matthew 19:14). How do you think Jesus feels about Halloween? If Jesus was sitting in your living room on October 31, would he encourage your children to go trick-or-treating? Jesus is the one who said, "If anyone causes one of these little ones who believe in me to sin, it would be better for him to have a large millstone hung around his neck and to be drowned in the depths of the sea" (Matthew 18:6). His desire is for the building up of children, not for their harm.

Protecting children. Albert James Dager presents the following argument against any participation in Halloween. Although we do not necessarily agree with everything he declares, he makes some strong points:

> As pastors and teachers have the responsibility of educating parents, the responsibility of educating children in the commandments of God weighs heavily upon the

shoulders of parents. But no more so in this age or society than in ages past. The difference is that today children rule many homes, Christian and non-Christian alike. For that reason, compromise is the easy way out for parents who, thinking they are showing love by acquiescence, are really destroying their children's spiritual life.

No matter what the evil, parents are forever searching for alternatives in order that their children not feel deprived of the world's fun. When it comes to Halloween, Christians decide to substitute their own parties for the world's. Instead of calling their festivities "Halloween parties," they call them "Harvest Festivals" and dress them in biblical costumes. But that's what Halloween is: a harvest festival. And many children wear biblical costumes for Halloween anyway, so what's the difference except in the compromise of their minds? You can be sure that to most children it's still Halloween that they're celebrating....

It isn't going to traumatize children if they aren't allowed to join in some things just because "everyone else is doing it." It's the responsibility of Christian parents to teach their children the truth from the beginning; not to wait until they've been sufficiently infected by the world that they must be deprogrammed at a later date. Children who are taught to love Jesus will understand that, because of that love, they shouldn't have anything to do with the celebration that glorifies the power of God's enemies.[2]

Teaching the light of Christ. Unfortunately, the Christian church never truly Christianized Halloween—the Roman church merely baptized it with its own unique, and many times unbiblical, beliefs concerning sin, the saints, and purgatory. We think the solution is for the Christian church to follow the lead of the Reformer

Martin Luther. Rather than condone or support the dark traditions of Halloween, let's strive to make Halloween a universal day to joyfully celebrate and teach the Reformation's principles and all it implies to us and our children. This especially includes the doctrines of Scripture alone (Scripture, not the church, as the final authority), faith alone (a relationship with God by grace through faith alone), and glory to God alone.

God's desire is that we teach our children truth, the light about Christ, rather than join in the dark practices of Halloween night. In Deuteronomy 4:5-10, Moses writes,

> See, I have taught you decrees and laws as the LORD my God commanded me, so that you may follow them in the land you are entering to take possession of it. Observe them carefully, for this will show your wisdom and understanding to the nations, who will hear about all these decrees and say, "Surely this great nation is a wise and understanding people." What other nation is so great as to have their gods near them the way the LORD our God is near us whenever we pray to him? And what other nation is so great as to have such righteous decrees and laws as this body of laws I am setting before you today?

> Only be careful, and watch yourselves closely so that you do not forget the things your eyes have seen or let them slip from your heart as long as you live. Teach them to your children and to their children after them. Remember the day you stood before the LORD your God at Horeb, when he said to me, "Assemble the people before me to hear my words so that they may learn to revere me as long as they live in the land and may teach them to their children."

In other words, just as the ancient Israelites could

offer a testimony of God before the surrounding nations by obeying and teaching the commandments of God—and by this glorify God before the nations—so Christians can do something similar on Halloween. By lifting up the teachings of Christ on Halloween, Christians can become a positive example to their neighbors around them concerning the greatness and power of God's Word to change lives and glorify the one true God.

Participate or not?

In summary, here are some things to consider concerning whether or not your children should participate in Halloween:

1. It is the most sacred day of many religions that are connected with evil spirits and Satan.

2. It was and is believed to be the day of the year on which the devil's help could especially be invoked for a variety of things; it remains a special day to Satanists.

3. Human sacrifice of children and adults has often been practiced on this day.

4. It has and will continue to encourage non-Christian spiritual activity on the part of both children and adults. Halloween is growing in popularity and decadence.

5. It is a special day to call on spirits through various spiritual practices that are often promoted as innocent fun. For example, children try out a Ouija board or participate in séances.

6. It is a day historically known for divination.

7. It helps support pagan philosophies and practices such as reincarnation, animism, shamanism, and Druidism.

8. It is of help to the practices and beliefs of mediums and psychic researchers by encouraging people's interest in things such as ghosts and poltergeists.

9. It can unequally yoke Christians and pagans (see 2 Corinthians 6:14).

10. It is likely that no Halloween activity or symbol can be found that does not go back to a non-Christian religious source.

11. Christian participation in Halloween can in many ways be dishonoring to God.

12. "Everything that does not *come from faith* is sin" (Romans 14:23).

Of course, when Halloween activities actually involve practices of witchcraft or paganism, the Bible is clear that these are sinful and to be strictly avoided. Both the Old and New Testaments have many references condemning the practice of witchcraft, sorcery, spiritism, contacting the dead, divination, and similar actions—all things imitated and associated with Halloween:

> Do not turn to mediums or seek out spiritists, for you will be defiled by them. I am the LORD your God (Leviticus 19:31).

> Let no one be found among you who sacrifices his son or daughter in the fire, who practices divination or sorcery, interprets omens, engages in witchcraft, or casts

spells, or who is a medium or spiritist or who consults the dead.... The nations you will dispossess listen to those who practice sorcery or divination. But as for you, the LORD your God has not permitted you to do so (Deuteronomy 18:10,11,14).

[King Manasseh of Judah] practiced sorcery, divination and witchcraft, and consulted mediums and spiritists. He did much evil in the eyes of the LORD, provoking him to anger (2 Chronicles 33:6).

Nowhere are we told such activities are acceptable before God. In light of these Scriptures, it is unreasonable to suggest that the Bible is accepting of such practices.[3]

Halloween, Haunted Houses, Poltergeists, and Witchcraft

6

What is the historic connection between Halloween and ghosts?

From its origins with the ancient Druids and their cult of death, the dominant theme of Halloween has been one of ghosts, spirits, and the dead. Lewis Spence reports,

> There is no doubt that the original idea underlying all these various ceremonials is that the spirits of the dead might be pacified and prevented from haunting the living. The festivals to the dead are among the earliest in the world...beginning with the idea of fear, and therefore of propitiation.[1]

The degree of influence of the spirits of the dead, ghosts, and poltergeists upon Halloween and related festivals around the world can be seen in literature and the media.

The influence of the supposed ghosts of the human dead on Halloween and, in fact, most religious traditions throughout the world, leads us into our next section. As we've mentioned, Halloween is assumed by many to be an innocent pastime, but some of the practices and phenomena associated with it need to be carefully evaluated. These issues are serious topics that require much more than the superficial approach often taken. By its historical associations and very nature, Halloween can lead people to a fascination and involvement with things like poltergeists and contemporary forms of witchcraft.

7

How are ghosts, haunted houses, and Halloween related?

The poltergeist is something that must be fought as well as investigated (D. Scott Rogo, psychical researcher).[2]

Ghosts, things that go bump in the night, spooks, poltergeists, and haunted houses are all part of Halloween. Even apart from Halloween, ghost stories are everywhere today. Literally dozens of television specials and segments on programs like *Unsolved Mysteries*, *The X-Files*, *Sightings*, *The Extraordinary*, and *Paranormal Borderline* have captivated millions of viewers. Urban myths and haunted house legends abound on the Internet.

Terror for a price

HauntedHouses.com offers a nationwide map of haunted houses and ghost towns for the serious fan. Haunted houses are sometimes even in demand, and some real-estate agents specialize in selling them to fascinated clients—at greatly inflated prices.[3]

Every Halloween, television programmers market a tempting lineup of supernatural thrillers on TV, such as the four in the Poltergeist series. Although Halloween comes and goes, interest in the phenomenon of the ghost or poltergeist remains all year long. Since the 1980s, poltergeist phenomena have also found their way into immensely popular movies such as the proto-typical ghost films *Ghost Busters* (1984), *Ghost Busters II* (1989), *Ghost Dad*, with Bill Cosby (1990), and *Ghost*, with Patrick Swayze (1990). More recent films, including *The Sixth Sense*, *White Noise*, *The Shunned House*, and *The Ring*, have added to this proliferation of the haunted-house genre. Even popular Christian fiction authors Ted Dekker and Frank Peretti have explored the haunted-house mystery from a Christian perspective through their book and film *House*.

In some ways, ghost and paranormal themes have begun to dominate Hollywood television. The 2005–2006 TV season, for example, included 14 pilots with supernatural themes.[4] One program, *Ghost Whisperer* (starring Jennifer Love Hewitt), portrays a woman who helps dead people deliver messages to people still living on earth, allowing the souls a final rest. The Sci-Fi Channel also hosts *Ghost Hunters*, a reality TV series that consists of two plumbers who travel around the United States to collect evidence of ghost activity via high-tech equipment. Several additional examples abound, including *Dead Tenants*, a show on the Learning Channel in which psychics help homeowners with ghost problems; *Dead Famous: Ghostly Encounters*, a Biography Channel series in which a pair of psychics track down famous dead spirits; and the two programs *America's Most Haunted Places* and *Haunted Hotels* on the Travel Channel.

The term *poltergeist* itself comes from two German words: *polter*, to make noise by throwing or tumbling around, and *geist*, ghost or spirit. The literal transla-tion of the term is "noisy ghost." These "noisy ghosts" are nothing new. Michael Goss compiled an annotated bibliography of over 1,000 English books on poltergeists during the period from 1880 to 1970. In his text he observes, "Poltergeists seem to have been plaguing the human race since the dawn of time and they have shown a grand impartiality as to the theatres of their operations. They are as much at home in the jungles of Indonesia as they are in the suburbs of London or the bustle of New York City." Throughout America, "Poltergeist experiences occur every day of the week."[5] Hardly anyone hasn't heard genuine ghost stories, but even among the millions who have personally experienced ghosts, few have any real idea as to what is actually happening.

8

What are the theories advanced to explain ghosts?

The theories put forth to explain or identify ghosts or poltergeists are almost as diverse as the phenomenon itself. Among these, poltergeists are suggested to be 1) the spirits of human dead; 2) unknown spirits; 3) demonic spirits or biblical demons; 4) spontaneous, uncontrollable outbursts of psychokinetic energy, usually associated with a young person emerging into adolescence; 5) various other manifestations of human "psychic" activity; 6) inexplicable phenomena resulting from anomalous and unidentified geophysical conditions (although this view is held by some noted rationalistically inclined psychic investigators, it is perhaps the least credible theory to those who have personally experienced poltergeist events); 7) consequences of the human spirit being projected or forced outside the body as in uncontrollable out-of-body experiences or "astral" projection; and 8) a post-mortem "vestige" of human personality somehow imbued with powers to affect the physical realm.

Of these, the three most common theories are

1. *the biblical viewpoint*—that poltergeists are demons;

2. *the mediumistic interpretation*—that poltergeists are the roaming spirits of the human dead; and

3. *the parapsychological view*—that poltergeists constitute an entirely human phenomenon and result from various manifestations of alleged psychic power.

Note that the last two interpretations justify certain pre-existing theories that are often passionately advocated by those who hold them. For example, in the mediumistic view, poltergeists provide alleged "evidence" that all spirits of the human dead may roam freely—and, thus, are not immediately confined to heaven or hell as the Bible teaches (see Matthew 25:46; Luke 16:19-30; 2 Peter 2:9; Revelation 20:10-15). This supports the non-Christian belief that men and women never die spiritually in the biblical sense of eternal separation from God. Rather, it is believed that, in general, the spirits of the human dead merely experience a normal transition into the next life, where they have the opportunity to continue their spiritual evolution based on individual merit earned in their previous life (or lives). This interpretation of ghosts is often combined with belief in reincarnation.

The parapsychological view interprets poltergeists in a different manner. Poltergeist phenomena are believed to result from alleged recurrent spontaneous psychokinesis (RSPK) of adolescents (usually females)—that is, from the alleged psychic powers of the human mind. This idea lends support to the cherished theory of innate human psychic potential long advocated by the parapsychological and New Age communities. For example, in ascribing poltergeist phenomena to human psychic power, the noted psychical researcher D. Scott Rogo commented, "In thinking about man's unwelcomed guests, the poltergeists, let us remember that our psychic abilities can plague as well as benefit us."[6]

However, some psychical researchers have also accepted the occult, mediumistic interpretation that these entities are troubled or confused ghosts or earth-bound spirits who, because of their supposed past life or lives on earth, have been hampered in their spiritual evolution. Rather than progress into higher spirit realms or the finer dimensions of the spiritual world, they remain aggressively attached to what they call the earth plane.

We find these last two theories unconvincing due to both the Bible's teachings and the nature and actions of poltergeists themselves. The mediumistic theory fails to answer the issue, because the Bible teaches that immediately after death the human dead are either with Christ in heaven or confined to punishment in hell and therefore unable to roam in the spirit world or haunt houses (Philippians 1:23; 2 Corinthians 5:6-8; Luke 16:22-26; 2 Peter 2:9). The parapsychological theory is not possible either, because the idea that human beings have genuine psychic powers that can generate ghosts is false.[7]

So how do we explain *real* ghosts?

9

Is the biblical view of ghosts credible in light of the facts surrounding hauntings and poltergeists?

The biblical view explains poltergeist phenomena as the result of the activities of evil spirits or demons. But does this theory make sense? Most serious paranormal researchers will hardly consider the idea, arguing along with Michael Goss that "there is no one theory which comfortably accounts for *all* poltergeist cases."[8]

However, this is not necessarily the case. The poltergeist phenomenon and its New Age spiritual connection offer strong empirical evidence for the demonic nature of these spirits. In fact, we have found *no* genuine poltergeist case that cannot be accounted for on the basis of this theory.

An uncomfortable idea

The demonic theory is often rejected today simply because mediums, parapsychologists, and others who research supernatural phenomena don't prefer it. In spite of the evidence and the explanatory power of the demonic theory, they choose to accept the view they personally feel comfortable in believing.

Two important observations need to be made. First, it is necessary to realize that poltergeist phenomena are *not* proof that any person supposedly psychically or otherwise associated with these events is spirit-possessed. The *person* is not causing the unusual phenomena. Again, this is an unfounded premise of the discipline of parapsychology. The poltergeist manifestations themselves are merely the result of an evil spirit working miraculous events around a person for ulterior motives.

Second, at least temporary *demonization* (also sometimes called *demon possession*) of individuals has occurred as a result of some poltergeist hauntings. But more often the people who experience poltergeists or are involved are simply victims—either intrigued or terrified, depending on the severity of the haunting.

We believe an evaluation of the poltergeist phenomenon itself will accomplish two things: 1) it will dispel parapsychological (psychokinetic) and naturalistic (hallucinogenic) theories as incomplete explanations; 2) it will dispel the mediumistic view by offering strong evidence that poltergeists are demons—not the confused spirits of dead people.

10

Do ghost phenomena require a supernatural explanation? And how are ghosts connected to demons?

Considered objectively, poltergeist phenomena are very difficult to explain apart from the supernatural. Theories of natural or human origin are simply inadequate in many instances.

Representative phenomena

Poltergeists involve an incredible number of diverse manifestations and unsavory incidents. These may include horrible foul smells, cold rooms, thick or oppressive air, unusual malevolent voices, bizarre, creaturely, or human apparitions, movement of objects (even very heavy ones), spontaneous fires, strange markings on furniture or people, headaches and other physical symptoms, and electromagnetic phenomena.

In his extensive bibliography, Michael Goss describes the following phenomena commonly associated with poltergeists. Even though the poltergeist has been named after its auditory effects, other phenomena may be included, such as the following:[9]

- Showers of stones, earth, mud, sticks, fruit, shells, and, occasionally, more bizarre material such as banknotes, small animals, and so on, may occur.

- Objects—for example, furniture—may be rolled, moved, overturned, or otherwise agitated; in particular, small items are likely to be thrown, levitated, caused to simulate a rocking or "dancing" motion, or may be swept across the room in flights of complicated and sustained trajectory from which they descend either gradually and gently in hovering motion or very abruptly.

- Bedclothes, linen, garments, and curtains may be molested, torn, slashed, or otherwise damaged. In some rare cases, linen has been found to have been deliberately arranged in the form of a "tableau" reminiscent of human figures at worship.

- Small objects may disappear from their appointed places, possibly making subsequent reappearances in highly incongruous situations...Others fail to reappear at all.

- "Apports" (objects perhaps foreign to the afflicted household) may similarly arrive on the scene.

- Manipulations suggestive of internal malfunction

may affect electrical equipment later found to be in normal working order. Telephones may ring or register calls when none have been made; plugs are removed and lightbulbs smashed or wrenched from their sockets.

- "Spontaneous" fires may break out.

- Pools or jets of water (or other liquids) may be emitted from normally dry surfaces—for example, walls, ceilings, and so on.

- Personal assaults, such as blows, slaps, shoves, etc., may be inflicted on householders and their guests. However, stigmata in the form of wheels, toothmarks, or scratches are likely to be confined to one particular person, namely the supposed "agent" or "focus" in the disturbances.

- Apparitions (human, animal, or indeterminate) are sometimes witnessed, as are unusual lights, clouds of phosphorescence, and so on.

- In a few instances, a form of psychic invasion characterized as "possession" or entrancement with associated psi abilities and the poltergeist agent has been reported.

As Raymond Bayless correctly reports, "With a poltergeist, every form of psychical phenomena both in the experimental séance and in spontaneous cases, has been reported, and the sheer diversity of manifestations is truly incredible. It is almost impossible to list all the strange, individual actions attributed to the poltergeist."[10]

The *Unsolved Mysteries* TV series, on February 23, 1996, reported that the famous Los Angeles Comedy

Store is subject to serious hauntings.[11] One waitress alone had chronicled at least 50 supernatural events. In the 1940s and 1950s, The Comedy Store was called Ciro's. It was the most popular nightclub in all Hollywood and widely considered "the place to be seen." Ciro's was frequented by famous movie stars such as Tyrone Power, Bette Davis, and Lucille Ball as well as by mob gangsters such as Mickey Coleman and Ben "Bugsy" Siegel, the murderous mobster who built The Flamingo, one of the earliest Las Vegas casinos.

Coleman allegedly killed a number of people at Ciro's. The story says these individuals continue to haunt The Comedy Store today. What is significant about the story is not the characteristic death connection in poltergeist events, which, as we saw, supposedly confirms there is no biblical judgment at death, but the kinds of events that have happened there. Consider two examples. In one case, in a matter of just a few seconds, all the table chairs in the mainstage room were piled in a heap one on top of another. An individual was in the room and all the chairs were neatly placed around the tables; he left the room for a few seconds and came back to find them all piled in a heap. Further, not a sound was heard.

In another incident, a waitress had just finished getting the room set up for the evening's performance. She had placed tablecloths over the tables, put down ashtrays, and so forth. She left the room for a few seconds, came back and, incredibly, found that the room was just as it was before she had fitted all the tables. In other words, in a matter of literally less than ten seconds, all the ashtrays, tablecloths, silverware, and napkins that had been on the tables were now lying in their original positions, waiting to be placed. The tablecloths and other items were *neatly* stacked.

Evil origins

Things like this could not be the result of a mental hallucination or psychokinesis, adolescent or otherwise—especially since no adolescents were present. (In fact, have those who advocate this strained theory of adolescents and psychokinetic energy ever done a credible study to determine just how frequently adolescents are even present at poltergeist events?)

In addition, in examining poltergeists as a whole, there are truly frightening apparitions that can only be characterized as demonic and which may seriously injure people. There are also reports of horrible encounters with beings which may take grotesque human form and in rare cases proceed to kill or sexually rape both men and women, leaving them covered with a slimy substance, terrible odor, or both.

A possibility?

The rare if controversial phenomenon of spontaneous human combustion—people instantaneously bursting into flames and being largely reduced to ashes—may have some kind of association with poltergeists.

And, as noted, there are also numerous examples of demonic possession occurring during poltergeist manifestations.[12] Thus, in many cases investigated, "the nature of the invading force has many times been annoying and malicious, and frequently has displayed a vicious and dangerous nature.... Poltergeist's intentions...were in the main savage, destructive and malignant."[13]

It is not surprising then, as paranormal authority Colin Wilson points out, that "until the mid-nineteenth century it was generally assumed that poltergeist disturbances were the result of witchcraft, or evil spirits, or both." In his bibliography, Goss points out in a similar fashion that earlier generations "concluded quite logically that they were faced by the work of witchcraft and/or demons" and that such a theory "has shown remarkable durability regardless of what the twentieth century may think about witchcraft and demons."[14]

In fact, researchers have connected the poltergeist to mediumism, witchcraft, spiritism, and other forms of the occult throughout history. Numerous incidents were recorded or investigated by the late Dr. Kurt Koch, a leading Christian authority on the issue. In his research, he concluded that in every case "occult practices lay at the root of the [poltergeist] phenomena."[15]

Indeed, poltergeists are connected with demonic spiritual practices, not hallucinations or adolescent psychokinesis. This connection is illustrated by the fact that the revival of spiritualism in America actually began with a poltergeist. The Fox sisters from Hydesville, New York, who are considered the founders of the spiritualism movement in the United States (1848), heard "rappings" that were clearly a manifestation of poltergeist activity. Colin Wilson, noted author of *The Occult: A History*, observes, "The Hydesville rappings which inaugurated the history of modern spiritualism were almost certainly poltergeist phenomena; the Hydesville 'ghost' also claimed to be the victim of an undetected murder."[16]

Once poltergeist disturbances are experienced in a home, often a Ouija board is brought out of a closet in an attempt, whether in seriousness or for fun, to establish contact with the so-called troubled ghost. In such cases, poltergeist phenomena often become the means of a person's conversion to believing in the spirit world. The supernatural encounters are so startling and intriguing that even initially skeptical observers may come to a belief in the supernatural and become involved in psychic investigation, such as seeking the advice of psychics, using automatic writing, or attending séances.

Poltergeist phenomena are frequently associated with necromancy (communicating with the dead) and séance phenomena as well. For example, "[The poltergeist] has duplicated every phenomenon observed in the experimental séance." And, "During known, obvious poltergeist cases, phantoms have been seen and heard that gave every indication of having been spirits of the dead. On occasion, phantoms have indicated that they were spirits of dead relatives of witnesses present."[17]

Necromancy

From a Christian view, we see this as a typical attempt by demons to establish belief in or practice of contacting the dead—something God has forbidden in the Bible (Deuteronomy 18:9-12). This is illustrated in the attempt to rescue supposedly confused or earthbound spirits who are allegedly causing the poltergeist disturbances. "In each case the living had a duty to the dead. By means of séances (sometimes specifically convened as 'rescue circles') the distressed party [the poltergeist] could be contacted and ultimately directed along the appointed paths of self-improvement."[18]

In fact, we suspect that in many cases where poltergeists *are* directly associated with some person rather than a location, demons are attempting to trick the individual into some kind of dark spiritual involvement or even bring about his or her possession.

At the least, when poltergeist phenomena seems to be associated with an individual, there are certain parallels to the medium and her spirit controls: "Obviously, this relates to the concept of mediumship in general and moreover to the equally fascinating study of the way in which this person—the 'agent' or 'focus'—is different from other human beings who do *not* have poltergeist abilities."[19]

In light of this, it is not surprising that a common feature of ghost or poltergeist manifestations involves the attempt to seek actual contact with the dead. This is also a common occurrence in séance mediumism. For example, I (John Weldon) remember viewing a television program on a particularly dramatic poltergeist haunting. After the poltergeist manifestations began, a Ouija board was used to attempt to make contact with the spirit. Through the board, the spirit spelled out its name to those present.

The next day psychical researchers were called in to investigate. Hauntingly, one of these parapsychologists had the name of this spirit mentally impressed upon him entirely without his knowledge. He simply began his conversation, "When did you first meet _____?" and gave the actual name that the spirit had given the day before through the Ouija board. He had no idea *why* he said this name or where it came from, but obviously it confirmed the "identity" of the spirit they were now seeking to establish contact with. Further, this particular name was, in fact, found to be the very same individual who had lived in that house prior to that time—and who had also been murdered. In the minds of everyone present, this confirmed the fact they were actually in contact with the deceased spirit of the man who had earlier been killed in this house. In these types of encounters, this kind of confirmatory scenario is not at all an uncommon occurrence.

11

Who do these ghosts claim to be? What are the consequences of believing in their common interpretation?

Ghosts or spirits (also called spirit guides), in general, are often contacted directly by psychics, mediums, or channelers. They permit themselves to become possessed by these spirits and allow those spirits to speak through them. At poltergeist hauntings, mediums or psychics may also allow themselves to be possessed in order to discover the alleged reason for the haunting by establishing direct contact with the troubled ghost. Of course, in these circles, the poltergeist is characteristically interpreted in line with prevailing beliefs about the dead and human psychokinesis. But given the well-known ability of demons to assume virtually any shape and to take virtually any disguise, from angels to UFO aliens to the human dead, how can mediums or others involved be certain that ghosts are what they think they are? Can mediums be certain the appearances of supposed dead loved ones in séances are not the clever tricks of demons to foster emotional trust and dependence?

Words from the "dead"

While speaking through human mediums, the ghosts that are contacted during poltergeist outbreaks have offered several reasons that explain their activities. First, some claim to be the spirits of the dead who were atheists, materialists, or rationalists while on earth and never expected to encounter an afterlife. Upon death, their shock was so great they became confused and disoriented. Like a lost and wounded traveler in a strange city, they wander aimlessly, attempting to get their bearings.

Second, some say ghosts are spirits confused otherwise. Initially, some spirits of the dead supposedly refuse to believe they are really dead and are no longer able to live upon the earth. They now vainly attempt to convince themselves they are still in their bodies and can somehow return to their previous existence. As a result, they not only seek to regain contact with the living through haunting houses where the living reside, but they desperately seek to manifest themselves materially in order to regain contact with the physical world. Bizarre poltergeist events are one result of their attempt to interact with and materialize back into their previous existence.

Third, some ghosts argue that they are alleged spirits of Christians who erroneously accepted the idea of a biblical heaven. They project the idea that they are shocked, dismayed, and angry to discover that the Bible they trusted was wrong. Rather than finding themselves in heaven with their Lord, they claim they have instead found themselves in the spirit world with no Jesus or heaven anywhere in sight. Some of the ghosts refuse to accept their condition and vent their confusion, anger, and grief through poltergeist manifestations.

Fourth, ghosts claim to be the spirits of the dead who were evil people involved in violent acts such as murder or rape at a particular location on earth. After death, they claim they have chosen to remain close to the earth to continue their evil. Or, they claim they are deceased victims of evil people and are frightened to go forward and progress spiritually, or they wish to seek revenge on the living relatives of those who harmed them.

Finally, ghosts may say they are the spirits of the dead

who are experiencing confusion resulting from suicide. Famous medium George Anderson, who communicated regularly with alleged spirits of the dead, mentioned the following anecdote concerning his personal friend. "A friend of mine who had recently taken his life came through [me] and did not know how to go into the light. I kept telling him to go forward to the light, but he was afraid of [temporary] judgment. He couldn't forgive himself. Also, he was having a problem with the fact that after he had taken his own life, his spirit obviously lingered around the scene of the act."[20]

These are the claims of ghosts and poltergeists. But regardless of the spirits' claims, we think the demonologists of an earlier era such as de Spina (1460), Nider (1470), Remy (1595), and Guazzo (1608) were correct: These spirits are not what they claim (spirits of the human dead), but are lying spirits the Bible identifies as demons. This is strongly indicated by the fact that ghost claims, manifestations, and results tend to have five distinct consequences—*all* of which lend major credibility to the Christian view.

Five dangerous results

The five consequences of accepting the common view that ghosts are the human dead or manifestations of human psychic ability are detailed in the following several pages.

1. Practices of spiritual darkness. As noted, ghost or poltergeist manifestations tend to involve or interest people in the practices of spiritual darkness. Poltergeist phenomena frequently cause unsuspecting people to assume the truth of alternative views such as mediumism, witchcraft, and reincarnation. The phenomenon itself is so startling that participants become converted to belief in the supernatural and, not infrequently, end up personally involved in psychic investigation through séances, channeling, Ouija boards, or various forms of divination. As a result, a parapsychologist may be called in to investigate the ghost or poltergeist disturbance. Often a psychic, channeler, or medium is brought in to communicate with the troubled spirit, to attempt to help it or, if it is evil, to exorcise it or cast it out.

Demons have a vested interest in all this because it offers a novel and unexpected manner for them to influence or contact people. Poltergeist activity encourages people to attempt to contact the dead—something God has forbidden and considers detestable, as noted previously:

> Let no one be found among you who…practices divination or sorcery…engages in witchcraft, or who casts spells, or who is a medium or spiritist or who consults the dead. Anyone who does these things is detestable to the LORD (Deuteronomy 18:10-12).

2. Discrediting the Bible's teaching. In the minds of many people, ghosts and poltergeist phenomena tend to discredit the biblical view of the afterlife and of immediate judgment at death. Indeed, most people in the world think of ghosts as the spirits of the human dead. But if these large numbers of dead are actually roaming around the spirit world and contacting our world, then the biblical portrait of the confinement and judgment of the unregenerate at death is obviously false.

This scenario also supports the goals of demons, who have a determined interest in deceiving people about biblical truth concerning the afterlife. For instance, if there is no hell in the afterlife, there is no need for a

Savior in this life. But God tells us, "Man is destined to die once, and after that to face judgment" (Hebrews 9:27). Those who reject God's gracious offer of salvation Jesus warned, "If you do not believe that I am [the one I claim to be], you will indeed die in your sins" (John 8:24, brackets in original).

The writer of Hebrews asks, "How shall we escape [judgment] if we ignore such a great salvation?" and "see to it that you do not refuse him who speaks. If they did not escape when they refused him [Moses] who warned them on earth, how much less will we, if we turn away from him [Jesus] who warns us from heaven?" (Hebrews 2:3; 12:25).

The Savior's words

Jesus himself emphasized that those who do not have a personal relationship with him "will go away to eternal punishment, but the righteous to eternal life" (Matthew 25:46).

The Bible teaches clearly that the unsaved dead are now confined in a place of punishment, while the saved dead are in glory with Christ (Luke 16:19-31; 2 Peter 2:9; Philippians 1:23; 2 Corinthians 5:6,8). Therefore, the inference most people draw from poltergeist manifestations—that the dead roam freely—is clearly inaccurate from a biblical viewpoint. Ghosts and poltergeists are evil spirits manifesting themselves to deceive and sometimes frighten people.

3. *Promoting trust in the demonic.* Ghost and poltergeist events grant spiritual authority and credibility first to the occultist (the psychic, spiritist, medium, channeler), and second to those involved with them (the parapsychologist, psychical, or paranormal researcher).

It is these individuals who investigate the disturbance and supposedly solve the problem. Because such persons are frequently able to resolve the disturbance, although usually not without a battle of sorts (with the spirits gladly cooperating behind the scenes), the entire episode grants those involved with these spirits, whether personally or supposedly scientifically, a good deal of spiritual prestige. But as many former mediums have revealed, such resolutions to ghost and poltergeist hauntings are merely a ruse of the spirits to fool people into adopting unbiblical teachings or practices.[21]

This is also something that harmonizes well with the goal of demons: to secure people's trust in those who, however unwittingly, actively promote the demons' own interests and often actively oppose Christianity. As the history of spiritual deception reveals, these activities hinder the good purposes God has intended for humanity.

4. Advocating human "psychic potential." Concerning the parapsychological view of poltergeist phenomena being a result of human psychic potential, this confuses the realm of the psychological and the supernatural, masks the activity of demons, and helps make the domain of the supernatural the domain of the psychologist. The popular adolescent theory suggests that when certain children approach the age of puberty, this somehow creates an excess amount of psychic energy which, in some unknown manner, is spontaneously released to create poltergeist effects. Poltergeist manifestations are presumed to indicate an abnormal condition of the human mind. This theory concludes that the true source of the poltergeist is found in the human psyche, a result of a mass of outwardly projected adolescent repression, fear, anger, or confusion.

One consequence of the idea that poltergeist phenomena mysteriously emerge from the consciousness of adolescents is to draw children and psychologists into the ranks of those who study poltergeist phenomena. As a result, the poltergeist becomes the natural domain of the psychologist and, from that point, the psychologist finds it easy to become entwined in the spiritual domain of the parapsychologist. In essence, the *psychological* theory inevitably links the poltergeist with the adolescent, the adolescent with the psychologist, and the psychologist with the parapsychologist.

This consequence can be seen in the attempt to make poltergeist phenomena of human origin. This, by definition, opens the doors to exploration of human psychic potential. As authority Colin Wilson remarks, "The recognition that poltergeists are of human origin was one of the greatest intellectual landmarks in human history. It was the first convincing proof that we possess other floors"[22] (meaning other psychic levels or dimensions within our own being).

Given the demonic nature of the poltergeist phenomena as a whole, it is hard to believe that so many otherwise rational people ascribe poltergeists to some kind of alleged spontaneous, uncontrollable, psychological, or psychic function of human beings. Yet parapsychologists, psychic researchers, and paranormal researchers who investigate these phenomena seem to consider the demonic theory hardly worthy of mention. But isn't the demonic theory far more believable than the idea that human psychic energy can account for the kinds of manifestations we find? To give more examples:

> Objects are projected with alarming velocity, and often seem directly aimed at some human target.... Another

peculiarity is the wavy path, quite irreconcilable with gravitational laws, which these projectiles often seem to follow. They turn corners, swerve in and out, and behave, in fact, like a bird which is free to pick its own way. Not less surprising is…that the stones and other missiles are for the most part invisible at the beginning of their flight. They do not come into view until they are just a few feet off. They enter closed rooms and seem to drop from the ceilings or to penetrate doors and windows without leaving a trace of their passage.[23]

What human being on earth, adolescent or aged, can duplicate such things? Indeed, it is the consistently supernatural nature of the phenomena that so forcefully argues *against* a purely human origin. This also advances the purpose of demons who, hiding safely behind the realms of the parapsychologist and the psychic simultaneously, promote antibiblical beliefs and redefine the demonic into a purely psychological realm.

5. *Hurting people*. Poltergeist manifestations frequently harm people either physically, emotionally, or spiritually. Therefore the view of poltergeists as harmless ghosts also plays into the hands of demons. Since demons are innately evil and unredeemable, this fits well with their own desires and purposes.

In essence, all five consequences of the poltergeist are seen to support the goals of those evil spirits the Bible identifies as demons. Therefore, it is hardly out of place to suggest that poltergeists are actually a plan of demons to further their own agendas.

12

Does Halloween support witchcraft?
Is witchcraft dangerous?
Are ghosts related to witchcraft?

Beyond the idea of roaming spirits of the dead, witchcraft is perhaps the most common theme of Halloween. However, our cultural image of witchcraft is changing from that of something evil to something innocent or even spiritually positive.

Proselytization and promotion

Leading former witch Doreen Irvine reports how the proselytizing activity of modern witches is designed to recast their tarnished image historically: "It was important to give witchcraft a new look, and these guidelines were laid down: 'never frighten anyone. Offer new realms of mystery and excitement. Make witchcraft less sinister. Make it look like a natural, innocent adventure...cover up evil with appealing wrappings...'"[24]

One way witches can deceive children is by recasting themselves in a positive light. Those involved in witchcraft often use Halloween to teach children that witchcraft is good and witches are genuinely spiritual people, healers, and protectors of the environment. Of course, most witches today claim to be good witches (also called white witches), which causes much confusion. From a biblical perspective all witchcraft is evil. Nevertheless, our culture increasingly recasts witchcraft and neopagan communities as those who would help both humanity and the planet Earth itself, even suggesting that witchcraft is compatible with biblical Christianity.

A *"positive" religion?* In *The Anatomy of Witchcraft*, Peter

Haining described leading witch Raymond Buckland as "certainly the most important Gardnerian witch in America and perhaps the cult's most level-headed and convincing spokesman."[25] I (John Weldon) had a radio debate with Buckland, who, in the early 1960s, was probably the individual most responsible for reintroducing modern-day witchcraft to the United States. He has written more than 30 books on various aspects of the subject. In our debate, Buckland claimed the following of witchcraft: "It's just another religion…it's not anti-Christian—it's nothing like that. The main message is positive…We hold pretty much the same ideas of doing good [as Christians]…I've spoken at Roman Catholic colleges on Long Island, New York, I've spoken for Methodists, for Baptists, for Episcopalians—many, many different groups. Generally, I would say that there's been a very good reaction: 'Now this is interesting. Tell us more.' That's the sort of reaction that I've gotten, rather than anything antagonistic."[26]

Buckland's view of witchcraft as something that is not anti-Christian but rather good and positive is contradicted by the facts, not to mention God's own view. In Scripture we are told very clearly that anyone who "engages in witchcraft…is detestable to the LORD" (Deuteronomy 18:10,12).

The recent trend of presenting witchcraft in a positive, benign light is part of the reason for the success of witchcraft in Western culture.

> Even back in 1999, the demographics of Wiccans in the United States [were] difficult to find. There is much to-do about secrecy, and groups do not release membership rolls. [Phyllis] Curott estimates there are 3 million to 5 million Wiccans. Helen Berger, associate professor of sociology at the University of Westchester

in Pennsylvania, has surveyed more than 2,000 Wiccans for her research. Estimates cited by Berger and Christian apologist Craig Hawkins in his book *Witchcraft: Exploring the World of Wicca* put the U.S. witch population at the 150,000 to 200,000 mark.[27]

Today, however, even some Christians don't seem very convinced about the dangers of witchcraft. One evangelical scholar claims, "The majority of witchcraft and ritual magic appear to be relatively innocuous," even going so far as to assert that ritual magic may be "essentially harmless."[28] Again, such attitudes are contradicted by the history of witchcraft, ritual magic, and the testimony of current and former practitioners. And certainly Halloween plays a significant part in this shift:

> In the opinion of Dr. David Enoch, former senior consultant psychiatrist at the Royal Liverpool Hospital and the University of Liverpool, Halloween practices open the door to the occult and can introduce forces into people's lives that they do not understand and often cannot combat…For too many children, this annual preoccupation…leads to a deepening fascination with the supernatural, witches and the possibility of exercising power over others.[29]

"*Good*" *witches?* As another example, consider the *Harper's* magazine article "Toward a more P.C. Halloween." It reproduces excerpts from the teacher's manual of the *Anti-Bias Curriculum: Tools for Empowering Young Children*, produced by the Anti-Bias Curriculum Task Force of Early Childhood Educators in California and published by the National Association for the Education of Young Children in Washington, D.C. In this manual we are told that the Halloween image of the witch as old, wicked, ugly, and dressed in black "reflects stereotypes of gender, race, and age: 'Powerful women are evil; old women are ugly and scary; the color black is evil.'" The myth of the evil witch "reflects a history of witchhunting and witch-burning...directed against mid-wives and other independent women."

P.C. witchcraft

We are told that the stereotype of witches as evil should be challenged today "because it is so offensive, especially to many women."

An example is given of a teacher named Kay, who has performed the following activities two weeks before Halloween. She first asks the children what they think about witches. She receives the standard responses of "bad, ugly, old." The teacher then says, "Many people do think that. What I know is that the real women we call witches aren't bad. They really helped people.... They healed people who were sick or hurt." This gets the children talking about doctors and the teacher replies, "Yes, the [witch] healers were like doctors."

On other days, Kay brings in various herbs showing how they were used by witches in healing and she also sets up a "witch-healer" table "where the children can make their own potions." At the end of the two-week course, children have a new consensus—that witches fall into two categories: "Some were bad, some good. So although the activities don't completely change the children's minds, they do stretch thinking by creating a category of 'some good witches.'"[30]

With the explosive growth of witchcraft in America and its growing influence in our general culture, the practices of witchcraft, such as potion-making, spell-casting, communicating with the dead, and divination, are being seen as innocent and even positive practices.

What is forgotten today is that witchcraft *is* increasingly appealing to a large number of people because of the manner in which it is presented along with the community and power it offers. For example, Guadalupe Rosales, a former witch, discusses why witchcraft was so appealing to her and has become so appealing to many others: "It all seemed so harmless and so beautiful. It was a beautiful experience…Wicca builds community. It builds community because there are so many people out there seeking this oneness with the earth, this oneness with the universe, this oneness with the ultimate god and goddess aspect. Everybody wants love, everybody wants to get along, everybody wants peace, and in Wicca, when you are involved in a group, it starts off that way."[31]

The dark and dangerous

Yet Guadalupe Rosales found a reality different from what she initially encountered. First, in contrast to the claims of Raymond Buckland that witchcraft is not anti-Christian, Rosales found just the opposite. Having a Christian background, she wanted to use Christ in her rituals. But the witchcraft council would not allow her to use the name of Christ—not even as one god among many. "They just said: 'No, you are forbidden to use Christ.'"[32] She was taken before the council several times for discussion or discipline.

Rosales also eventually found that there was a great deal of envy and animosity among her coven members. And in the end, she reports,

> I saw it all for what it really was when I was trying to leave and separate myself from them. They made it hard for me.

I had nightmares and visions that nobody else had and sicknesses that were not accounted for physically.... I was being pressured into going into the art of necromancy, which is raising of the dead in witchcraft....

It is just too dangerous in both a spiritual sense and a mental sense. If you are not strong enough spiritually, it will drive you crazy...I had to make a choice. It was either witchcraft or God....

To this day, almost two years later, I am still being followed. I am still being attacked on and off. I think the worst came a couple of weeks ago. I ran into this person that appeared to be demonized, on the street, and she threatened my children. She said that if I did not go back [into witchcraft] my children were going to die by the 12th of this month.... It is now after that date. I was hit pretty bad. I was sick and there was a point of stagnation where I just could not seem to move. I had no will of my own but I had much prayer through the churches and I prayed myself.... Praise God my children are now fine.[33]

She soberly tells her former witch friends that should they, too, cross the line, "You will come to the conclusion that the people you thought loved you the most, that took you into the craft, your best friends, have become your worst enemies."

Certainly witchcraft is no harmless pastime, and the use of Halloween to encourage witchcraft is terribly misguided. Rosales also recalls, "As a witch you always seem to seek the counsel of a spirit guide."[34] Raymond Buckland, quoted earlier, says that the focus of witchcraft is "a belief in deities, and a worship of these deities, thanking them for what we have, asking them for what we need."[35]

Involvement with the powers of evil

Witchcraft, poltergeists, and other forms of spiritism tend to go hand-in-hand. Biblically, this means that witchcraft is involved with what the Bible calls powers of darkness. If these spirits and ghosts are really demons, no other conclusion is possible.

Montague Summers's *Geography of Witchcraft* and *History of Witchcraft*, as well as many standard encyclopedias and compendiums on witchcraft, show the close connections between witchcraft and poltergeists. Consider the following discussion by leading occult authority Colin Wilson in his book *Poltergeists: A Study in Destructive Haunting*. He discusses the historical connection between witchcraft, poltergeists, necromancy, and spiritism and points out that writing the text of an illustrated book about witchcraft "proved to be an excellent preparation for writing a book about poltergeists."

> And *all* witchcraft has been based on the idea of magic: that the witch or magician can make use of spirit entities to carry out her will…The chief business of a witch in those days (about 1,000 B.C.) was *raising the dead*. And later tales of witches—in Horace, Apuleius and Lucan—make it clear that this was still true 1,000 years later on. After the beginning of the Christian era… the witch also became the invoker of demons…. In his notorious *History of Witchcraft*, the Reverend Montague Summers denounces modern Spiritualism as a revival of witchcraft. He may simply have meant to be uncomplimentary about Spiritualism; but, as it happens, he was historically correct. The kind of spiritualism initiated by the Fox sisters was the nearest approach to what Lucan's Erichtho, or Dame Alice Kyteler, would have understood by witchcraft. It begins and ends with the idea that we are surrounded by invisible spirits, including those of the

dead, and that these can be used for magical purposes.... Witchcraft is about "spirits"—the kind of spirits we have been discussing in this book.[36]

In conclusion, Halloween, poltergeists, witchcraft, and spiritism are all closely connected. This means that however innocent Halloween may be at one level, at another level its innocence is lost altogether. Further, because of the modern revival of witchcraft and other forms of neopaganism, an article on the subject in *Christianity Today* correctly reports that

> profound changes are underway in the religious climate of the West. They suggest that new religious forces are nibbling at the foundations of a society and a culture built largely upon a Christian worldview.[37]

This is certainly the case. Due to these influences, Christians must be counted on now more than ever to stand for God's truth amidst a culture facing such spiritually dark forces.

Closing Remarks from the Authors

If you have not yet made the decision to follow Jesus Christ as your personal Lord and Savior, or if you have recently experienced the dark power of witchcraft or the supernatural and desire to find the true God and eternal life (1 John 5:13), we would encourage you to sincerely pray the following prayer:

> Lord Jesus Christ, I *humbly acknowledge* that I have sinned in my thinking, speaking, and acting, that I am guilty of deliberate wrongdoing, that my sins have separated me from your holy presence, and that I am helpless to commend myself to you. I *firmly believe* that you died on the cross for my sins, bearing them in your own body and suffering in my place the condemnation they deserved. I *have thoughtfully counted the cost of following you*. I sincerely repent, turning away from my past sins. I am willing to surrender to you as my Lord and Master. Help me not to be ashamed of you. *So now I come to you*. I believe that for a long time you have been patiently standing outside the door knocking. I now open the door. Come in, Lord Jesus, and be my Savior and my Lord forever. Amen.[38]

Becoming a follower of Christ is a serious commitment. We encourage you to find an understandable translation of the Bible and begin to read it for yourself, especially the New Testament. Also, we would encourage you to begin to pray daily in your new relationship with Christ. Another way to grow in your faith is to find other followers of Christ to meet with for regular spiritual growth in a Bible study or local Bible-teaching church.

We hope this resource has been a help to you. To share your story or personal decision, or provide other feedback on this book, please contact us at

factson@johnankerberg.org

or write us at

The Ankerberg Theological Research Institute
PO Box 8977
Chattanooga, TN 37414

A Brief Timeline of Halloween

1000 BC and previous   Pre-Christian Celts celebrate November 1 as their New Year (Samhain) and practice the night before as the evening where the veil between the living and the dead was opened.

AD 43   The Romans conquer the Celts and the Roman harvest festival, Pomona (celebrated on November 1), eventually merges with Samhain.

609 or 610   Pope Boniface IV designates November 1 as All Saints' Day.

835   Pope Gregory III rules that All Saints' Day always falls on the same day as Samhain. He also declares that young men can go door to door to collect food for the poor and that villagers can dress in costumes as saints to celebrate the holiday.

1517   On October 31, Martin Luther posts the 95 Theses on the door of the Wittenberg Church.

1600s   New England Puritans ban Halloween since it is Catholic in origin. Only Catholics and Episcopalians continue to observe the holiday.

1840s   A surge in Irish immigration to the United States sparks growth in Halloween traditions.

1912   The Dennison Manufacturing Company begins publishing Halloween books with party, decoration, and costume ideas. (It first began publishing Halloween materials in 1909.)

1921   Anoka, Minnesota, becomes the first American city to officially sanction Halloween as a holiday.

1923   New York City begins Halloween celebrations.

1925   Los Angeles begins citywide Halloween celebrations.

2004   The Puyallup, Washington, school district bans Halloween from schools out of fear of offending local Wiccans.[39]

NOTES

Trick or Treat?

1. Mary Bellis, "Halloween 2006 Promises Big Business," *About.com*, October 23, 2006. Accessed at http://inventors.about.com/b/a/257301.htm.

2. "Trick-or-treaters Can Expect Mom or Dad's Favorites in their Bags This Year," National Confectioners Association, 2005. Accessed at www.candyusa.org/Media/Seasonal/Halloween/pr_2005.asp; "Fun Facts: Halloween," National Confectioners Association, 2004. Accessed at www.candyusa.org/Classroom/Facts/default.asp?Fact=Halloween.

3. Melinda Fulmer, "These Days, Halloween's a Big Deal," MoneyCentral.com, 2006. Accessed at http://articles.moneycentral.msn.com/CollegeAndFamily/Advice/TheseDaysHalloweensABigDeal.aspx.

4. Fulmer.

5. "President Proclaims 'National Magic Week,'" *MagicTimes Press Wire*, September 12, 2000. Accessed at www.magictimes.com/archives/2000/pr20000912a.htm.

6. "Halloween Office Party," Socreepy.com, 2006. Accessed at www.socreepy.com/halloween-office-party/.

Section One: Halloween—Ancient, Medieval, and Modern

1. Ruth Hutchison and Ruth Adams, *Every Day's a Holiday* (New York: Harper & Brothers, 1951), p. 235.

2. Some facts about the Druids are disputed or uncertain; there are geographical peculiarities plus differences between early and late Druidism.

3. "Celtic Religion," *Encyclopaedia Britannica Macropaedia*, vol. 3., p. 1068.

4. "Celtic Religion," pp. 1069-70.

5. For more, see John Ankerberg and John Weldon, "What Is the Occult?" at http://johnankerberg.org/hp-articles/hp-occult-def.htm or *The Facts on the Occult* (Eugene, OR: Harvest House, 1991).

6. Julius Caesar, *Commentaries*, book 6, chapter 18.

7. Becky Stevens Cordello, *Celebrations* (Butterick Publishing, 1977), p. 112.

8. Lewis Spence, *The History and Origins of Druidism* (London: Thorson, n.d.), p. 99.

9. Robert J. Myers, *Celebrations: The Complete Book of American Holidays* (Garden City, New York: Doubleday & Co., 1972), p. 259.

10. "Halloween," *Encyclopaedia Britannica Macropaedia*, vol. 4.

11. See Cordello, p. 114.

12. Myers, p. 260.

13. Carol Barkin and Elizabeth James, *The Holiday Handbook* (New York: Clarion, 1994), p. 41.

14. Myers, p. 261.

15. Father Andy Costello, "Sin Is a Boomerang," *U.S. Catholic*, Nov. 1992, pp. 37-38; George William Douglas, *The American Book of Days* (New York: H.W. Wilson, 1938), p. 548.

16. Despite Catholic claims, the best defense of purgatory is found in only a few verses in a noninspired text, 2 Maccabees 12:41-45, which 1) does not mention purgatory and 2) rejects Catholic doctrine by teaching the deliverance of soldiers who had died in the mortal (hence unforgivable) sin of idolatry. Bible verses alleged to support the doctrine require an extremely forced exegesis. In his *Systematic Theology* (1974, p. 687), Louis Berkhof writes, "The doctrine finds absolutely no support in Scripture, and moreover, rests on several false premises, including the insufficiency of Christ's atonement; that our good works are meritorious before God; and that the Church can shorten or terminate purgatorial sufferings." Compare John Ankerberg and John Weldon, *Catholics and Protestants* (Chattanooga, TN: Ankerberg Theological Research Institute, 1994), pp. 192-94.

17. John Ankerberg and John Weldon, *The Facts on Roman Catholicism* (Eugene, OR: Harvest House, 2003).

18. Ethel L. Urlin, *Festivals, Holy Days and Saints' Days: A Study in Origins and Survivals in Church Ceremonies and Secular Customs* (London: Simpkin, Marshall Hamilton, Kent & Co., 1915; reprint ed. Detroit: Gale Research Co., 1979), p. 201.

19. Costello, p. 39, 37.

20. Myers, p. 258.

21. Urlin, p. 201.

22. Urlin, p. 198.

23. Dorothy Gladys Spicer, *Festivals of Western Europe* (New York: H.W. Wilson, 1958), p. 17.

24. Margaret Read MacDonald, ed., *The Folklore of World Holidays* (Detroit: Gale Research, Inc., 1992), p. 521.

25. MacDonald.

26. Spicer, p. 47.

27. Hutchison and Adams, p. 236.

28. Gail S. Cleere, "Halfway to Winter," *Natural History*, Oct. 1992, p. 74.

29. George William Douglas, *The American Book of Days* (New York: H.W. Wilson, 1983), pp. 544-45.

30. Cordello, p. 119.

31. Joseph Gaer, *Holidays Around the World* (Boston: Little Brown & Co., 1955), pp. 155-56.

32. MacDonald, p. 520.

33. Hutchison and Adams, p. 236.

34. Douglas, p. 542; Myers, p. 262.

35. Douglas, p. 542.

36. Myers, p. 259. Douglas, p. 542.

37. Douglas.

38. MacDonald, p. 520.

39. Douglas, p. 539.

40. Sue Ellen Thompson and Barbara W. Carlson, comp., *Holidays, Festivals, and Celebrations of the World Dictionary* (Detroit, MI: Omnigraphics, Inc., 1994), p. 132; current information on the Voodoo Museum is available at http://voodoo museum.com; Jennifer DeCoursey, "Monster Event for Marketers," *Advertising Age*, Oct. 16, 1993, p. 41.

41. Margot Adler, *Drawing Down the Moon: Witches, Druids, Goddess-worshipers, and other Pagans in America Today* (New York: The Viking Press, 1979), p. 108.

42. "School Says Halloween Disrespectful to Witches," *ABC News*, October 21, 2004. Accessed at http://abcnews.go.com/US/story?id=184701.

43. Costello, p. 38.

44. The divergent emphasis on nature and Satan, respectively, differences in ritual, and so on, cannot obscure the commonalities in source of power, psychic development, anti-Christian worldview, use of spirits, use of evil, and so on. Further, any serious study of biblical demonology will reveal Satan as the power behind false religion, witchcraft, idolatry, and the occult.

45. Doreen Irvine, *Freed from Witchcraft* (Nashville, Thomas Nelson, 1973), pp. 94-95.

46. We make no claim regarding any specific occurrence on this issue, but only mention that it has been alleged in association with Satanist groups. See Nigel Davies, *Human Sacrifice: In History and Today* (New York: Harper Collins, 1981); Terry Maury, *The Ultimate Evil* (New York: Barnes & Noble, Inc., 1999); Larry Kahaner, *Cults That Kill* (New York: Random House, 1988); Dawn Perlmutter, "The Forensics of Sacrifice: A Symbolic Analysis of Ritualistic Crime," *Anthropoetics*, Fall 2003/Winter 2004, Institute for the Research of Organized and Ritual Violence, www.anthropoetics.ucla.edu.ap0902/sacrifice.htm; State of California, Office of Criminal Justice, "Occult Crimes: A Law-Enforcement Primer" Sacramento, CA: Winter 1989-90.

47. Lewis Spence, *The History and Origins of Druidism* (London: Aquarian Press, 1971), pp. 104ff; "Celtic Religion," *Encyclopaedia Britannica Macropaedia, vol. 3*, p. 1069.

48. Spence, p. 159; compare *Encyclopedia Britannica Macropaedia*, p. 1069.

Section Two: A Christian and Biblical Analysis of Halloween

1. Albert James Dager, "Halloween: Should Christians Be Apart?" *Media Spotlight*, 1986, PO Box 1288, Costa Mesa, CA 92628-1288.

2. Dager.

3. See John Ankerberg and John Weldon, *The Coming Darkness* (Eugene, OR: Harvest House Publishers, 1993), appendix A.

Section Three: Halloween, Haunted Houses, Poltergeists, and Witchcraft

1. Lewis Spence, *The History and Origins of Druidism* (London: Thorson, n.d.), pp. 104-09.

2. D. Scott Rogo, *The Poltergeist Experience* (New York: Penguin Books, 1979), p. 40.

3. Holden Lewis, "Want to Buy a Haunted House?" Bankrate.com, July 31, 2006. Accessed at www.bankrate.com/brm/news/mortgages/20021031a.asp.

4. Ron Rhodes, *The Truth Behind Ghosts, Mediums, and Psychic Phenomena* (Eugene, OR: Harvest House, 2006), p. 21.

5. Michael Goss, comp., *Poltergeists: An Annotated Bibliography of Works in English, Circa 1880–1970* (Metuchen, NJ: Scarecrow, 1979), p. vii; Robert Curran, *The Haunted: One Family's Nightmare* (New York: St. Martins Press, 1988), p. 101.

6. Rogo, p. 284.

7. We presented the evidence for this more extensively in our book *Cult Watch* (Eugene, OR: Harvest House Publishers, 1991), pages 257-281.

8. Michael Goss, comp., *Poltergeists: An Annotated Bibliography of Works in English, Circa 1880–1970* (Metuchen, NJ: Scarecrow, 1979), p. vii.

9. Goss pp. iii-iv.

10. Raymond Bayless, *The Enigma of the Poltergeist* (West Nyack, New York: Parker, 1967), p. 2.

11. Comedy stars such as Arsenio Hall, Roseanne, and Jim Carrey first got their start here.

12. See Rogo, p. 284, and Curran, pp. 114-17, 226-27; see, for example, Bayless, pp. 158-74.

13. Bayless, p. 159.

14. Colin Wilson, *Mysteries: An Investigation into the Occult, the Paranormal and the Supernatural* (New York: G.P. Putnam's Sons, 1978), p. 461; Goss, p. viii.

15. Kurt Koch, *Christian Counseling and Occultism* (Grand Rapids: Kregel Publishers, 1982), p. 181.

16. Wilson, pp. 462-63.

17. Wilson, p. 9, p. 205.

18. Goss, p. ix.

19. Goss, p. xii.

20. Joel Martin and Patricia Romanowski, *We Don't Die: George Anderson's Conversations with the Other Side* (New York: Berkeley Books, 1989), p. 242.

21. For more information, read former medium Ralphael Gasson's *The Challenging Counterfeit* and Robert Curran's *The Haunted: One Family's Nightmare*.

22. Wilson, p. 493.

23. Herbert Thurston, *Ghosts and Poltergeists* (Chicago: Henry Regnery, 1954), pp. 346-47.

24. Doreen Irvine, *Freed from Witchcraft* (Nashville: Thomas Nelson, 1973), pp. 101-02.

25. Peter Haining, *The Anatomy of Witchcraft* (New York: Taplinger, 1972), p. 93.

26. "Getting Serious About Witchcraft in America," interview with John Weldon and Raymond Buckland, *Rutherford* magazine, Aug. 1994, pp. 16-18.

27. Catherine Edwards, "Wicca Casts Spell on Teen-age Girls" *Insight on the News* magazine (online), October 25, 1999. Phyllis Curott is an attorney and the author of *The Book of Shadows*.

28. I. Hexham, "Satanism and Witchcraft" in *Evangelical Dictionary of Theology*, Walter A. Elwell, ed. (Grand Rapids: Baker Book House, 1984), p. 974.

29. Russ Parker, *Battling the Occult* (Downers Grove, IL: InterVarsity Press, 1990), p. 35.

30. "Toward a More P.C. Halloween," excerpts from the *Anti-Bias Curriculum: Tools for Empowering Young Children* by Louise Derman-Sparks and the Anti-Bias Curriculum Task Force, as given in *Harper's* magazine, October 1991, pp. 19, 21.

31. Aida Besancon Spencer, et al., *The Goddess Revival* (Grand Rapids: Baker Book House, 1995), pp. 198-199.

32. Spencer, et al., p. 200.

33. Spencer, et al., pp. 200-01.

34. Spencer, et al., p. 203.

35. "Getting Serious," p. 17.

36. Colin Wilson, *Poltergeist!: A Study in Destructive Haunting* (New York: Wideview/Perigee, 1981), pp. 319; 320-21.

37. Dave Bass, "Drawing Down the Moon," *Christianity Today*, April 29, 1991, p. 14.

38. Taken from John Stott, *Becoming a Christian* (Downers Grove, IL: InterVarsity Press, 1950), p. 25.

39. A special thanks to the Web site www.twoop.com/holidays/archives/2005/10/halloween.html for pointing out many of these key dates.

Asking tough questions...Offering real answers

Mission Statement

The Ankerberg Theological Research Institute (ATRI) is a Christian media organization designed to investigate and answer today's critical questions concerning issues of spirituality, popular culture, and comparative religions.

> *"But in your hearts set apart Christ as Lord. Always be prepared to give an answer to everyone who asks you to give the reason for the hope that you have. But do this with gentleness and respect, keeping a clear conscience, so that those who speak maliciously against your good behavior in Christ may be ashamed of their slander."*

—1 Peter 3:15-16

ATRI utilizes five strategies to accomplish this mission:

- *The John Ankerberg Show.* Our weekly half-hour TV program reaches over 147 million people in the U.S., in addition to millions more worldwide via satellite. The award-winning *John Ankerberg Show* is considered the longest-running and most-established television program available today providing answers to issues of importance to Christians (also called apologetics). Its documentary specials have been featured as nationwide television specials.

- *ATRI Radio*. ATRI reaches thousands of people through its one-hour weekend program and new one-minute daily radio commentary that is being offered on over 130 stations nationwide.

- *JohnAnkerberg.org*. ATRI's Web site reaches nearly 3 million unique visitors per year from 184 countries, providing a truly global impact. ATRI continues to utilize today's newest media formats as well, including online audio and video downloads, podcasts, blogs, and mobile technologies.

- *ATRI Resources*. In addition to over 84 combined published books and 2.5 million books sold by ATRI authors in several languages, its resources include over 2,500 online articles that have been utilized as research by some of today's best known media and academic organizations, both Christian and mainstream. In addition, ATRI offers transcripts of its TV interviews, which include thousands of hours of material from the past 28 years with top religious scholars.

- *ATRI Events*. Past speaking engagements have included Promise Keepers events, Focus on the Family seminars, and the National Apologetics Conference. Founder Dr. John Ankerberg has personally spoken to over one million people during his speaking and seminars in dozens of countries spanning five continents.

Due to ATRI's advanced research and long-standing work, founder and president Dr. John Ankerberg is regularly quoted in both Christian and mainstream media, including NBC, ABC, Daystar, and INSP, and has even testified before the U.S. Congressional Subcommittee on Financial Accountability for Christian Non-profit Organizations. A board member for many Christian media organizations, Dr. Ankerberg also serves on the board of directors for the National Religious Broadcasters Association (NRB).

THE FACTS ON SERIES
John Ankerberg and John Weldon,
with Dillon Burroughs

*To read a sample chapter of these or other Harvest House books,
go to www.harvesthousepublishers.com*

Understanding Neopaganism, Wicca, and Modern Witchcraft

WITCHCRAFT GOES MAINSTREAM
Brooks Alexander

The Halloween witch is dead. The old crone on a broomstick is gone. In her place is a young, hip, sexually magnetic woman who worships a goddess and practices socially acceptable magic.

As witchcraft goes mainstream, this new image, or some other aspect of the rapidly growing pagan religious movement, shapes the identity of more and more of your co-workers and neighbors... perhaps even your friends and family members. What do you do— what do you say—when you or your children meet someone like this?

Brooks Alexander, founder of the Spiritual Counterfeits Project, pointedly answers the tough questions:

- What do modern witches believe? Are they really following ancient pagan traditions or worshipping the devil?

- What's the real history behind Wicca and neopaganism? What can you learn from witchcraft's past?

- How might these spiritual beliefs transform our culture in the future?

- What does the widespread acceptance of witchcraft mean for you right now?

- How can you respond to protect your loved ones and reach out with the love of Jesus?

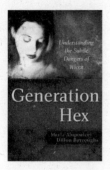

GENERATION HEX
Understanding the Subtle Dangers of Wicca
Marla Alupoaicei and Dillon Burroughs

Wicca is America's fastest-growing religion. By the year 2012, it's projected to be the third largest religion in the United States.

In *Generation Hex*, Marla Alupoaicei and Dillon Burroughs help you understand the spiritual hunger of a generation seeking truth, authenticity, and hope in a fragmented world. They consult practitioners of leading neopagan conferences in the Pacific Northwest and Canada, interview travelers to historic Salem, Massachusetts, and dialogue with several current and former adherents of Wicca and other forms of witchcraft, giving you the tools to evaluate the past and present of this growing spiritual tradition.

You'll be informed and equipped to understand Wiccan and New Age teachings, practices, and culture, especially if you're a parent. You'll also gain confidence in explaining this belief system to others and communicating the gospel to those caught up in it.

Great for personal study or as a gift for anyone interested or involved in Wicca.

To read a sample chapter of these or other Harvest House books, go to www.harvesthousepublishers.com